CAPITAL GROWTH

What the 2012 London Church Census Reveals

Capital Growth

What the 2012 London Church Census Reveals

Peter Brierley

Publishers
2013

ADBC Publishers,
The Old Post Office,
1, Thorpe Avenue, Tonbridge,
Kent TN10 4PW
United Kingdom

www.brierleyconsultancy.com

First published November, 2013

Cover design by David McNeill, Revo Creative
Maps drawn by Kim Tainio

Edited by Charlotte Hubback

Typeset by Graham Stacey, Orange and Blue

Printed in Great Britain by Bell & Bain, Glasgow

ISBN-13: 978-0-9566577-6-3

Dedication

To my wife of nearly 50 years, Cherry,
without whose constant support,
encouragement and willingness to
help in every way possible, this
analysis would never have been
finished nor the book completed.
She has been totally wonderful!

THANKS

So many have helped with this study. The original willingness of Dr John Nicholls, Chief Executive of the London City Mission, who both commissioned the study and had huge enthusiasm for the project ever after, always in meetings bringing an enormous breadth of understanding and keenness for church planting and the evangelism they represented, has been a constant source of inspiration. I would also like to thank John Marcus for his computer expertise, absolutely crucial to the project, Kim Tainio for both wrestling with SPSS to obtain the many analyses and drawing all the maps (not once but twice), Lynn Allen and a small team including Viv Concannon for filling and posting thousands of letters, Lynn for seemingly endless data input, Charlotte Hubback for very thorough editing, and many others involved in every possible way. While the mistakes remain my responsibility, the project as a whole to bring this to a successful conclusion is the work of many committed people, to all of whom a HUGE vote of thanks!

Contents

	Foreword	1
	Executive Summary	3
	Introduction	9
1	A Growing Number of Churches	19
2	London's Religions from the Population Census	35
3	Churchgoing in London	53
4	Age and Gender of London's Churchgoers	77
5	Churches and their Leadership	97
6	Church Activities	115
7	Church Planting	133
	The Challenges of the Census	145
	Appendix: Additional Tables	151
	Notes	159
	About Brierley Consultancy	165
	Index	167

Foreword

As a child, I sometimes heard my mother sing Hubert Gregg's wartime song, "Maybe it's because I'm a Londoner, that I love London so", although it wasn't strictly true in her case as she lived in Suffolk the first 18 years of her life, but subsequently lived in London for more than 70 years.

My father, however, was a true Londoner, being born in Plumstead and living in south London all his life (apart from his service in the First World War when he survived the trenches and the Battle of the Somme). My parents lived in the same house in Shooters Hill, Plumstead for 65 years. I was born and raised in London, and apart from two years studying theology at what is now the International Christian College in Glasgow and a few years teaching in Southampton, I have spent more than 60 years of my life in the Greater London area.

My father's ability at Euclid (the way that geometry was taught before WWI) must be in my genes, and when I went to school at Eltham College in south London, maths was the only subject I seemed able to understand, and love, and still do. Although it was suggested I become an actuary, I was guided into studying statistics; I've always been grateful for the training UCL gave me, and for the love of numbers my maths master, George Higgins, inspired.

In 1983, I became responsible for MARC Europe (now defunct), whose purpose was to strengthen church leadership, one aspect of which was providing research data hopefully to help leaders improve their strategic decision-making. Four Censuses of the English Church followed (and four in other countries too) so when the opportunity came in 2011, in discussion with Rev Dr John Nicholls, the chief executive of London City Mission, to undertake a Census of all the churches in London, I rejoiced. My love of statistical analysis and my love of London could be combined into a single goal, potentially for the good of the church.

The result is a unique look at the churches in the city of Greater London, detailed in the following pages. I hope you will enjoy reading it, and, if you are a church leader, you will find strength for your strategies, vigour for your vision and guidance for your growth, as you see what God is doing in this great metropolis.

Peter Brierley
August 2013

Executive Summary

In 2011 the London City Mission commissioned a London Church Census to take place the following year on 14 October 2012. It showed an estimated 720,000 people were attending church on a Sunday across London's 4,800 churches, or 9% of the population. These figures showed a considerable increase in the number of churches since the previous study (part of a country-wide Census in 2005), up 17% from 4,100 churches, and in the number of attenders, up 16% by 100,000 from 620,000 in 2005.

The London church scene, however, is complex. Over the last few years, both the number of churches and the number of churchgoers have increased substantially, and both far more than the rest of England. There are two particular groups of churches and churchgoers which, while not unique to London, are important because of their numbers – Black Churches and other Immigrant Churches, and Larger Churches (basically those with congregations in excess of 200, but often in excess of 500 people, including both adults and children).

Three groups of churches

About a quarter (27%) of all London's churches or congregations are in the "Black" or "Immigrant" category, the specifically black churches usually being called the Black Majority Churches (BMCs). These churches account for about a quarter (24%) of all churchgoers. It is these churches which have seen a considerable number of new plants in the last few years and a substantial increase in numbers attending, especially in some of the Inner London Boroughs. Half the attendance (48%) in Inner London in 2012 was black, up from 44% in 2005, while in Outer London it was less (21%).

The second group, Larger churches, also accounts for about a quarter (23%) of all the churches in London, but, because of their size, these naturally attract large numbers, and account for just over half of all of London's churchgoers (54%). These percentages include some large black churches as well. This group is also growing in terms of the number of churches and the number of attenders.

This leaves the third group, all the other churches, which together total half (50%) of all the congregations in London, but only account for a quarter of all the churchgoers (22%). This group has seen a number of churches close and the overall numbers attending decrease, and it is likely this trend will continue, so that the suggested numbers for 2020, eight years after the 2012 Census, could be still more congregations (a 5% increase is anticipated) but fewer people actually attending (a 2% decrease is suggested).

Immigration is a key factor

These figures can be broken down by denomination and churchmanship, but the picture is complicated by other significant factors, one of which is the huge number of immigrants who have come to London in the last decade and this trend is likely to continue. Chapter 2 analyses the government Population Census figures, which show that while, overall, some 9% of London's population attend church on a Sunday, this varies from 8% of the white population to 16% of the Chinese, Korean and Japanese population and 19% of the black population. Black attendance is especially strong in Inner London (17% of the population) and Asians in Outer London (20% of the population), but only 4% of those from the Indian subcontinent attend church (as many of these are Muslim). The combined Asian and Black population in London is 31% of the total, against only 8% in the rest of England. Many different languages are spoken across the city, and one of the growth points has been churches specifically catering for particular nationalities and languages.

Many of the Black churches have started in the close vicinity to where likely attenders live, while others, focussing perhaps on a specific language, see large numbers travelling to them (easy to do in central London).

Churchmanship

A further factor coming out of the strong Pentecostal and Evangelical (especially Anglican) presence in London is that some three-fifths of the churches are Evangelical (61%), as are half of the worshippers (52%). London is different from the rest of England, which in 2005 had 38% of both churches and attenders as Evangelical.

Churches of Catholic churchmanship account for 13% of churches but 27% of worshippers, because so many of the Roman Catholic churches are large. In addition, 5% of churches are Anglo-Catholic, accounting for 3% of worshippers. Some 11% of churches are Broad or Liberal, and 9% of worshippers.

Age and gender

Gender is a significant factor on the London church scene in two ways: more men under 20 attend church than women (29% against 24% of their respective totals). Also, of those joining the church between 2005 and 2012, four-fifths were women and only one fifth were men. While a quarter (25%) of churches have no-one at all attending under the age of 20, the percentage is almost double this (46%) across England.

The age composition of London churchgoers is also crucial – a third (32%) of London's churchgoers are aged between 20 and 44, compared with 20% in the rest of England. A third of all those attending church throughout England in their 20s are attending a church in London, and, of these, three-fifths attend a church in Inner London, and these mostly in the Boroughs of Camden, City of London, City of Westminster, Islington and Tower Hamlets. Larger, Pentecostal and Evangelical churches had more younger people attending than other churches.

Ministers and their churches

Many churches started in London in the second half of the twentieth century. Leadership is always an important factor, and 7% of ministers were responsible for more than one church (against 32% across England). Two-thirds (67%) of churches had a paid ordained leader, but only 13% a paid full- or part-time youth worker. Anglican and New Churches were more likely to have youth workers than other denominations. The leader* was likely to stay in post longer than in other parts of the country.

Half the churches had just one service on a Sunday, a third had two, and a fifth (19%) three or more. One church in seven translated their services into a language other than English. Of attenders in new churches, 6% originally came from another religion.

Three-fifths (63%) of Pentecostal and New Churches rented their church premises, a third of those for all of Sunday. Two-fifths of churches shared their building with other churches. Three-quarters had a programme of community engagement.

London churchgoers were more likely to attend every week than elsewhere, and the proportion of visitors was marginally higher. A huge extra number of people was reported to attend at Christmas. Churchgoers had been attending the same church on average for 10 years and lived two miles away, less in Outer London than Inner London where people were able to travel more easily. Two-thirds (70%) were estimated to be active or regular members, 22% committed but not active, and 8% not yet committed.

Mid-week activities

Three-fifths (63%) of London churches had mid-week worship

*In this book "church leader" refers to the minister or priest or vicar with responsibility for (usually one) church or congregation or parish. The term "senior church leader" normally refers to a bishop, moderator, chairman etc. who has responsibility for a number of churches or congregations or parishes (large or small).

activities, especially Pentecostal, Roman Catholic and Anglican churches; some of these were lunch-time services. Average attendance at these was twice those in similar services in England generally in 2005 (55 to 29 people). Half (45%) of the churches had some kind of mid-week youth ministry, and a quarter (23%) had mid-week activities for others.

The overall impact of such was that some 308,000 people came to London churches mid-week, of whom almost two-fifths (38%) came only mid-week, boosting total weekly attendance to 840,000 people, or 10% of London's population. Sunday attendance was 720,000.

Church planting

One church in seven, 15%, had started another church within the last 20 years, with 93% of these still meeting. Pentecostals had started the most, followed by the Anglicans and Smaller denominations (most of the latter being specialist immigrant churches). Two-fifths were started by an individual or small group, and a third as an offshoot from a mother congregation.

Half of the respondents said a particular organisation, or person or other resource had been a major influence. Half started with a full-time leadership, on average eight years younger than existing church leaders. Average initial budget was £25,000. Churches were started for particular nationalities, or in specific locations, or to reach certain kinds of people, including adherents of particular denominations.

By the time a church was five years old, three-quarters (77%) had seen their congregation grow, about half seeing it double, but a few a very large increase. Two-fifths (38%) of the growth was reckoned to be new people, or at least those not previously churchgoers. Three-quarters said the new church was financially self-supporting after five years.

INTRODUCTION

London is:

- The capital of the UK.
- Home to 8 million people in the inner area, 14 million in the greater metropolis.
- A world city.
- A leading financial centre, yet its financial services account for only 9% of the local economy.
- Chosen by over 100 of Europe's 500 largest companies as their headquarters.
- The digital capital of the world.
- The most visited city in terms of international visitors (New York has more but many of them are Americans).
- The only city in the world so far to host the Olympic games three times.
- The only UK county to see church attendance increase significantly in the twenty-first century.

London has:

- The highest GDP of any European city.
- The busiest urban airspace.
- 43 universities and degree-awarding colleges.
- More students than anywhere in Europe.
- More orchestras than New York.
- More museums than Paris.
- The most-visited modern art gallery in the world (Tate Modern).
- The most popular music venue in the world (the O2 Arena).
- A significant, and growing, number of apprentices (16,000 in 2010, 50,000 in 2012).
- Bankers who pay £31 billion a year in government taxes.[1]
- Nearly 4,800 churches, including 1,000 Anglican and 1,500 Pentecostal.

A Brief History

The Romans first invaded Britain in 55 BC; Julius Caesar repeated his feat the following summer, but the main invasion was under Emperor Claudius in 43 AD who successfully occupied the south-east of England. David Potter notes, "The Romans took another 50 years to firmly establish their ascendancy over the majority of the country and to quell opposition from native tribes."[2] A large-scale revolt in 60 AD by Boudicca almost completely destroyed Colchester, St Albans and London (or Londinium as the Romans called it). Subsequently the Romans consolidated their power, and London expanded. The Emperor Constantine "Christianised" the Roman Empire; prior to his elevation he lived in Britain.

In 407 the Roman occupation of Britain ended and London subsequently rapidly declined. In Anglo-Saxon times, London was part of the Kingdom of Essex. In 604 London received Bishop Mellitus, who founded the first St Paul's Cathedral. Viking attacks meant Danish dominance until this was ended by King Alfred the Great in 886. For safety, people moved within the old Roman walls, which were repaired, and the bridge rebuilt, with a second fortified Borough established at Southwark. From this point, the City of London began to develop its own unique local government.[3] In 1066, the victorious King William was crowned in Westminster Abbey.

London grew substantially after that. William built castles (including the Tower of London) and churches. A new bridge (that would last 600 years) was finished in 1209. Trade flourished during the Middle Ages and London consequently expanded. Its population in 1100 was 15,000, but by 1300 it had reached 80,000. During the Reformation, London was initially the principal centre for Protestantism in England. Henry VIII's dissolution of the monasteries saw much London property change hands. The population, reduced by the Black Death and other illnesses,[4] was 50,000 in 1530 but rose to 225,000 by 1605, augmented by the influx of a great number of immigrants. The plague in 1665 and the Great Fire in 1666 killed 60,000 people, one fifth of the then population. Sir Christopher Wren completed the new St Paul's Cathedral in 1710. The Bank of England began towards the end of the seventeenth century, and Lloyd's, the insurance underwriters, was founded.

During the eighteenth century, London rapidly enlarged its boundaries. The Industrial Revolution was beginning; crime was soaring. The nineteenth century saw London become the world's largest capital, and the centre of the British Empire; as a consequence many more immigrants arrived.[5] Some 2,200 churches were built (see Figure 5.1), a 50% increase over the number built the previous century. Tower Bridge, Big Ben and the Houses of Parliament, Trafalgar Square and many other landmarks were also constructed. The Great Exhibition was held in 1851. London became the financial centre of the world. In contrast, the twentieth century has seen aerial bombardment and terrorist attacks. The city is alive with history; from Lincoln's Inn, which can be traced back to 1422, and the Dominican Blackfriars of the thirteenth century,[6] to the historic Billy Graham Crusade of 1954, and to the Eye and Gherkin of recent years; the tallest building in Europe, the Shard, completed in 2012 above London Bridge station. Such large buildings, says one commentator, "are the vision of globalisation".[7] It has also hosted significant occasions such as the Queen's Diamond Jubilee, and annual international sporting events such as Wimbledon.

Church life and the Christian faith interweave into this cultural complex in a thousand ways, which makes the evaluation of one key section of the metropolis so fascinating. And not just Christianity, but many other religions too as Table 2.3 shows. London is continuing to change, with the present Coalition government committed to devolving power to local authorities through its localism agenda.[8] Some authorities are planning 50 years ahead with regard to housing and energy.[9]

What will happen to the population in future? Currently, it is 8.3 million (2011 Population Census), which the Office of National Statistics in 2010 predicted could rise to over 10 million by 2035, although the Greater London Authority put it at 9.3 million in 2011.[10] As the population grows, congestion is bound to increase (vehicles enter the Blackwall tunnel at the rate of one per second; if one breaks down a 600-vehicle queue forms within 10 minutes). Will increasing transport problems inhibit the growth of the church? As affordable housing continues to decline, will that impact it too?[11] Many such questions could be asked.

In 2013 London was the second most expensive city in the world, but notwithstanding it continues to undergo substantial development, such as at Nine Elms in Battersea, with possible Tube extensions.[12] Can the church in London continue to develop and take advantage of such changes? What is the church like in London today? It is time to look at the results of the 2012 Census.

The 2012 London Church Census

2012 was an exceptional year for London! It was the centre of the celebrations of the Diamond Jubilee of Queen Elizabeth II, with a magnificent flotilla of more than 1,000 ships sailing up the Thames, a lead boat ringing the bells from Richmond right through to the raised Tower Bridge. "We'll do it specially for the Queen," said the engineer in charge of the bridge machinery.

It also hosted the Olympic Games for a third time, made memorable not only by the incredible tally of 65 medals (third in world rankings) but also by the brilliant opening ceremony, created by Danny Boyle. The Paralympics followed with equally successful performances by so many, for the first time giving the Paralympics a significance on a par with the able-bodied Games.

It was also the year for the London Church Census. In June a letter was mailed to 4,500 churches across London advising the leaders of the forthcoming Census, and asking if any new churches were known to have started locally which might not be on our database. There was an excellent response to this and the final mailing in September with the Census form was sent to just over 4,800 (although as it happened some of these proved to be out-of-date). Altogether, the number of churches in London, after much research on the web, came to a total of 4,791. The Diocese of London was kind enough to supply a complete list of its churches and its most recent data for each, and, with extrapolations from the results of previous studies, numerical information was available in total from 2,588 churches, 54% of the number approached.[13] This percentage is higher than that achieved in the 1979, 1998 and 2005 English Church Censuses, but not quite as good as in the 1989 Census. Even so, by current professional response rates, it is an excellent percentage, and means the results rest on a robust base.

The Census took place on Sunday, 14 October, but if churches had something special on that day making it untypical for any reason, an alternative Sunday was chosen in October (or, for a few, in November) instead. A copy of the Census form is given in the book *UK Church Statistics* 2010-2020 [abbreviated to *Church Statistics*] which also contains some of the longer tables (most giving Borough detail) in its London Church Census section.

Council of Reference

The Census was backed by a Council of Reference to whom we are extremely grateful for their support. It consisted of the following people:

Beth Allen, Clerk, Six Weeks Meeting of the Religious Society of Friends
Revd Dr Kenneth Brownell, Senior Minister, East London Tabernacle, FIEC
Steve Clifford, General Director, Evangelical Alliance
Revd Canon John Coles, Director, New Wine
Rt Revd Stephen Cottrell, Bishop of the Church of England Diocese of Chelmsford
Rt Revd Graham Cray, Archbishops' Missioner and Team Leader of Fresh Expressions
Capt Terry Drummond, CA, Bishop's Adviser on Urban and Public Policy, Diocese of Southwark
Revd John Dunnett, General Director, CPAS
Lt Col Melvin Fincham, Divisional Commander, London Central Division, Salvation Army
Revd Canon Bob Fyffe, General Secretary, Churches Together in Britain & Ireland
Revd Stephen Gaukroger, Board Chair, Crossing London 2013
Mark Harding, Board Chair, London City Mission
Pastor Agu Irukwu, Head of the Executive Council, Redeemed Christian Church of God in the UK and Ireland, and Senior Pastor, Jesus House
Rt Revd Jana Jeruma-Grinberga, Bishop of the Lutheran Church in Great Britain
Revd Stuart Jordan, Chair of the London District, Methodist Church
Dr Tim Keller, Senior Minister, Redeemer Presbyterian Church, New York
The Most Revd Vincent Nichols, Archbishop of the Roman Catholic Diocese of Westminster
Revd Siew Huat Ong, Senior Minister, Chinese Church in London

Revd Roberta Rominger, General Secretary, United Reformed Church
Bishop Wilton R Powell, OBE, National Overseer, Church of God of Prophecy
Dr Neil Summerton CB, Chair of Partnership (Christian Brethren)
The Most Revd Gregorios Theocharous, Archbishop of the Greek Orthodox Archdiocese of Thyateira and Great Britain.

Bishop Wilton Powell was kind enough to give his endorsement of the Census for which we were very grateful:

CHURCH of GOD of PROPHECY

NATIONAL OFFICE
6 Beacon Court • Birmingham Road • Great Barr • Birmingham • England B43 6NN

Tel: +44(0) 121 358 2231 • Fax: +44(0) 121 358 8617
Email: admin@cogop.org.uk • Website: www.cogop.org.uk

ENDORSEMENT: London Church Census

I am in full support of the aims and objectives of the London Church Census. It is vital that the Church posses the crucial intelligence of the demographic shifts, which are impacting its intention for missions in London. An effective strategic response by the Church to meet the needs of our community is founded upon sound interpretive research with strong vision building facilitation.

Bishop Wilton Powell, OBE
NAITONAL OVERSEER
Church of God of Prophecy UK

Registered Charity No. 287868
Company Registration No. 1751385

Denominational Analysis

The results were all computerised and then analysed using SPSS software. As with all surveys there is inevitably a sampling error, normally estimated on a typical response of 50% within 95% confidence limits. In this case the range is 4%.

There are many denominations within the churches of London. Some 83 were separately classified, but this does not include numerous African and other national churches (which for simplicity were put together in a common group). The broad spectrum of denominations was, however, divided into 10 main sections as follows:

Anglican (99% of which are Church of England, ½% Free Church of England and ½% military chapels).
Baptist (79% of which are Baptist Union, 11% Grace Baptist, 2% Gospel Standard and 8% independent Baptists).
Roman Catholic (99½% of which are the Roman Catholic Church of England and Wales, with one Old Roman Catholic Church and one Tridentine Institute church).
Independent (30% are Christian Brethren [Open], 21% are FIEC [Fellowship of Independent Evangelical Churches], 4% are Congregational Federation, 4% Fellowship of Churches of Christ, 2% Evangelical Fellowship of Congregational Churches, 2% Christian Brethren [Exclusive] and 37% other independent churches).
Methodist (all of which are part of the Methodist Church of Great Britain. The Free and Independent Methodists don't seem to have any churches in London).
New Churches (24% are, or were, part of the Ichthus Christian Fellowship, 18% were part of c.net, 11% were Newfrontiers, 8% were part of Pioneer, and 39% part of other small House Church networks). New Churches are kept separately from other Independent churches for comparison reasons, even though most of the former networks in this category have now dissolved.
Orthodox (47% of which are Greek Orthodox and the remainder spread across several different nationalities).

Pentecostal (49% known African and West Indian churches, 13% Elim Pentecostal churches, 5% Assemblies of God, 4% Church of God of Prophecy, 3% New Testament Church of God, 2% Redeemed Christian Church of God, 2% Church of Pentecost, 1% Mountain of Fire churches, 1% United Pentecostal Church of Great Britain, and 20% numerous other smaller denominations).

United Reformed Church [URC] (99% URC and ½% Free Church of Scotland and ½% Evangelical Presbyterian Church in England and Wales).

Smaller Denominations (29% overseas national [immigrant] churches, 20% Salvation Army, 15% Seventh-Day Adventists, 12% Local Ecumenical Partnership [LEP] churches, 9% Religious Society of Friends meetings [Quakers], 8% Lutheran churches and 7% schools and hospitals holding regular Sunday services).

1

A Growing Number of Churches

One of the key features of life in London is the growing number of churches. Walk down Lewisham High Street and above one of the Indian restaurants is a room where an African church is advertised as meeting there every Sunday. The following week, likely as not, there'll be a similar sign in a room above another corner shop advertising perhaps a Spanish or Lithuanian church. Churches are proliferating, at the rate of two new churches every week – a rate which has continued for more than seven years.

The number of churches in Inner and Outer London is shown in Figure 1.1 (the data for which is in Table A1 in the Appendix), and it is obvious the number is increasing in both areas, but faster in Inner than in Outer London (between 1979 and 2012 the number in Inner London increased by 67%, and in Outer London by 25%). The actual number in Inner London is almost as many as in Outer London in 2012. The rate of growth in both areas, and thus in London as a whole, has been greater in the last seven years than previously, but this rate of expansion is expected to slow down (partly because of consolidation, and also partly because many new immigrant churches have already started and now are simply growing), to perhaps just one new church a fortnight on average over the next eight years, so that, by 2020, the total number of churches might be 5,030, with Inner London having a few more than Outer London.

Figure 1.1: Number of churches in London, 1979-2020E

Inner London · Outer London · Total

Borough Growth

Tables in *Church Statistics* give the details of the number of churches in each London Borough by denomination for 2005 and 2012. Some Boroughs have seen more rapid growth than others, which may be seen in Figure 1.2.

Figure 1.2: Growth in Number of Churches by Borough,2005 to 2012

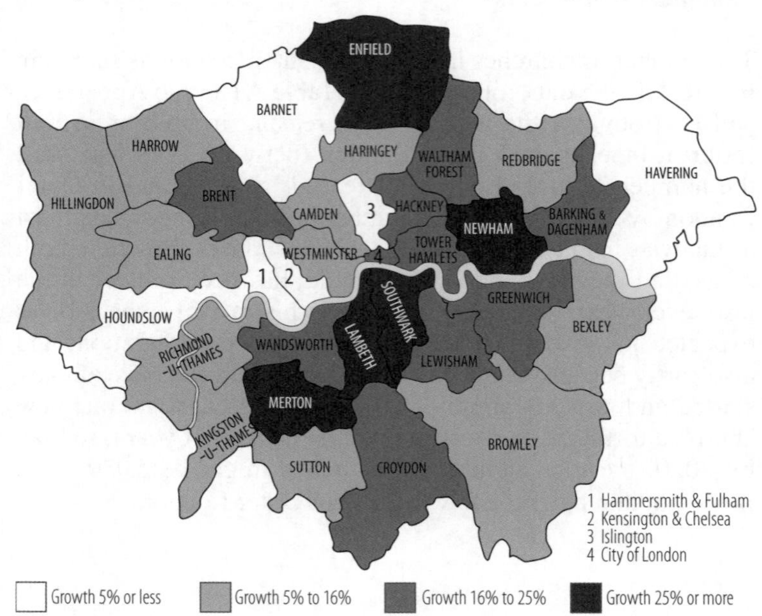

Three Inner London Boroughs have shown more than a 25% increase in the number of churches between 2005 and 2012: a remarkable rate of growth. These are Lambeth, Southwark and Newham, and also two Outer London Boroughs, Enfield and Merton. Five further Inner London Boroughs saw church numbers grow by between 16 and 25% – the City of London, Hackney, Lewisham, Tower Hamlets and Wandsworth, meaning 8 out of the 14 Inner London Boroughs saw exceptional growth. This but reflects the broad immigration pattern and the location of many black people, as these are often the ones starting new churches. It simply confirms new churches are frequently planted within a short distance of where possible attenders live, an issue to which we will return, as it is obviously important for church planting. Through experience the Redeemed Christian Church of God has learnt to establish churches "within ten minutes walking distance" of those it expects to attend, a factor of Nigerian church life where the denomination began.

However, this is only part of the story, as we shall see. Since the Pentecostals have started the largest number of new churches, many of those in Figure 1.2 are Pentecostal. Figure 1.3 shows the location of the existing Pentecostal churches, and an examination of both maps shows many of the new Pentecostal churches are in areas where there are already substantial numbers of churches. There is also tentative evidence to suggest some wider view of evangelism – the Boroughs of Enfield and Merton, for example, have seen a number of new churches started, two Boroughs where existing numbers are relatively low.

There were six Boroughs which saw very little increase in the number of churches – three in Inner London (Hammersmith and Fulham, Islington and Kensington and Chelsea) and three in Outer London (Barnet and Hounslow, while Havering saw a small drop in numbers – of two churches). There is a concentration of Jews in Barnet, but that is probably irrelevant to the fact that only five new churches were started there.

Figure 1.3: Number of Pentecostal Churches in London, 2012

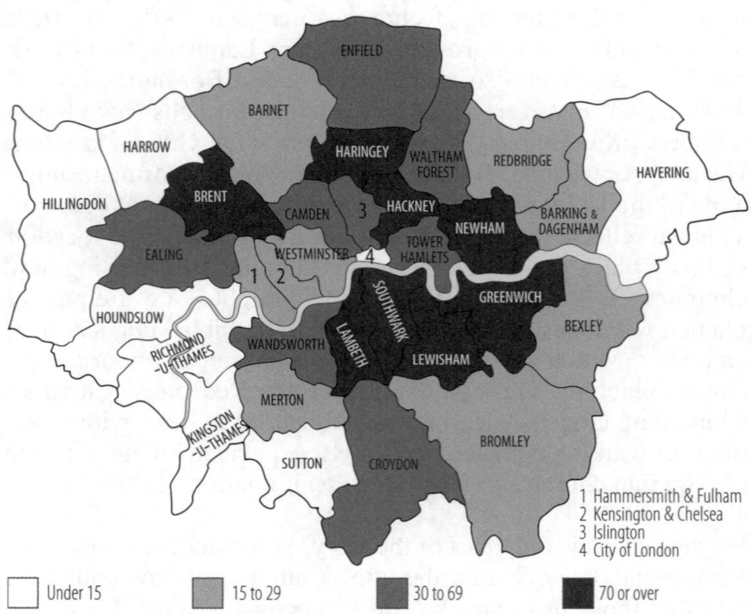

The project Being Built Together has been undertaken by a number of organisations including the University of Roehampton, Churches Together in South London and Southwark for Jesus, looking especially at the Black Majority Churches [BMCs] in the Borough of Southwark.[14] It concluded in June 2013, when they published their Final Report. They indicate there could be 140 BMCs in the Borough, whereas the Census gives a figure of 131. On the other hand, the Census gives more churches of other denominations, showing how hard it is to be certain that the numbers of churches are correct, despite diligent combing of lists and web research. The Being Built Together Report discusses the opportunities and planning issues faced by BMCs, and describes some of the community work they do, giving an excellent overview of BMCs in Southwark.

Denominational change

Table 1.4 shows the changing numbers of churches by

denomination across London.[15]

Table 1.4: Number of London churches by Denomination, 1979-2012

Denominations	Anglican	Baptist	Roman Catholic	Independent	Methodist	New Ch'es	Orthodox	Pentecostal	URC	Smaller Denom's	Total
1979 Total	982	270	434	276	253	76	31	596	183	249	3,350
1989 Total	987	287	422	292	252	142	51	709	174	243	3,559
1998 Total	991	355	417	264	253	269	79	875	162	197	3,862
2005 Total	1,017	368	411	307	251	253	94	1,005	152	229	4,087
% change 05-12	*+1%*	*-1%*	*-7%*	*+12%*	*-8%*	*+8%*	*-16%*	*+44%*	*-5%*	*+117%*	*+17%*
No opened	46	8	0	48	0	26	0	488	0	284	900
No closed	32	11	30	27	4	9	15	43	8	17	196
2012 Total	**1,031**	**365**	**381**	**328**	**231**	**270**	**79**	**1,450**	**144**	**496**	**4,791**
2020E Total	1,037	370	364	351	226	258	84	1,657	136	547	5,030

Over the 33 years to 2012 represented by this Table, the Anglicans have slowly but steadily increased their number of their churches in London, while the Roman Catholics and the URC have declined. The number of Baptist and Orthodox churches have also increased, except in the last seven years. Independent and Pentecostal churches have grown, the latter substantially. The number of Methodist churches has been static, except for the most recent period. New Churches have also generally increased. The Smaller Denominations declined in the first 19 years but have increased since, and after 2005 have more than doubled.

It may also be seen from Table 1.4 that some churches have closed as well as new ones opening. These numbers are estimates based on known information supplied by returned mail, current leaders indicating the closure of local churches, and the need to balance the overall figures. Inevitably, they are approximate and will exclude, for example, any churches which have both opened and closed in the years between 2005 and 2012. The year in which the closed churches originally opened is unknown in most cases, but it could be that the number of closures in this period is closer to a total of 300, rather than 200,[16] thereby making the number opened closer to 1,000 than 900.[17]

The number of closures puts the overall gains into some sort of perspective. Of the 4,087 churches in London in 2005, some 5% had closed by 2012, one church in 20. The denominational group with the largest number of closures – the Pentecostals – also had the largest number of openings, indicating growth comes with a price. All denominations have seen some closures. In only five of the 10 denominations do openings exceed closures.

Some of the closures shown for Orthodox churches are the result of a rationalisation of communities recorded in their annual Year Book. Chapels which were part of an existing church but had its own leader, used to be recorded as a separate building, and this practice has been discontinued. Likewise private chapels where there are no regular services are no longer included. The "closures" recorded therefore are more administrative adjustments rather than a loss of places of worship. Hence the increase in the estimated 2020 line as some Orthodox denominations are opening new worship centres.

Equally, it may be seen that while clearly there has been much energetic and visionary activity among the churches in London, half the new churches opened have been Pentecostal and more than a quarter are immigrant or Smaller Denominational churches. These are the two major growth engines in the capital.

The projected figures for 2020 come mostly from an extrapolation of existing trends over the last decades. They suggest the Anglicans, Baptists, Independent and Orthodox denominations will continue to plant more churches than they close, but the Roman Catholics, Methodists and URC will continue to close some. The Pentecostals will continue to plant churches but at a much slower net rate (and there may well be more closures than between 2005 and 2012).[18] New Churches may struggle to grow, while the increase in Smaller Denominations – the immigrant churches – will slow markedly as the church needs of existing immigrants are already being met. Will immigrants become more secularised as they are influenced by current British culture, and, therefore, lose the religious dynamism with which they arrived, and thus some of their churches close?

Ethnic and Immigrant Increase

The Pentecostal increase is almost entirely due to the number of Black Majority Churches [BMCs] which have grown especially in Camden, Hackney, Haringey, Lambeth, Lewisham, Newham, Southwark and Wandsworth in Inner London, and in Bexley, Brent, Croydon, Enfield, Greenwich, Merton and Waltham Forest in Outer London – in 15 of London's 33 Boroughs.

The Smaller Denominations increase is almost entirely due to the huge number of "Overseas National Churches" started, both Roman Catholic and Protestant, largely because of the number of immigrants coming to the UK (over the last decade especially), many of whom initially come to London, and many of whom stay there. This diversity can be readily seen in the ethnic grouping of London's population. Table 1.5 compares London's ethnicity with the percentages across the whole of England and Wales, taken from the 2011 Population Census:

Table 1.5: Ethnic groups of the Population, 2011

						Asian					Black			
Group:	W %	As %	B %	M %	0 %	I %	P %	Ba %	Ch %	0 %	Af %	Ca %	0 %	Base 100%
London	60	18	13	6	3	6	3	3	1	5	7	4	2	8.2 m
Inner	57	16	17	6	4	3	2	5	2	4	9	5	3	3.2 m
Outer	62	20	11	4	3	9	3	1	1	6	6	4	1	5.0 m
Rest of Eng'd	90	6	2	2	0	2	2	½	½	1	1	½	½	44.8 m
All England	86	8	3	2	1	3	2	1	1	1	2	1	0	53.0 m

W=White. As=Asian. B=Black. M=Mixed. 0=Other. I=Indian. P=Pakistani. Ba=Bangladeshi. Ch=Chinese Af=Affican. Ca=Caribbean. Eng'd=England

It is obvious from Table 1.5 that two-fifths of London's population is non-white, a proportion four times as great as that prevailing in the rest of England (40% to 10%). London has three times more Asians (18% to 6%), three times more "Mixed"

(6% to 2%) and six times more Black people (13% to 2%) than the rest of England.[19] The Asian numbers also show this: there are more Indians (6% to 2%), Bangladeshis (3% to ½%), and Others (5% to 1%), the last including Koreans, Japanese and Filipinos especially. Black people, Africans, Caribbeans, and West Indians, are much more prevalent within London than outside London.

Within London itself, the two lines "Inner" and "Outer" show many more black people live in Inner London – especially Africans. More Asians, on the other hand, live in Outer London, particularly Indians and "Other" Asians. Figures 1.6 and 1.7 use these 2011 Population Census figures to illustrate the location of Africans and Caribbeans.

Figure 1.6: Where Africans live in London

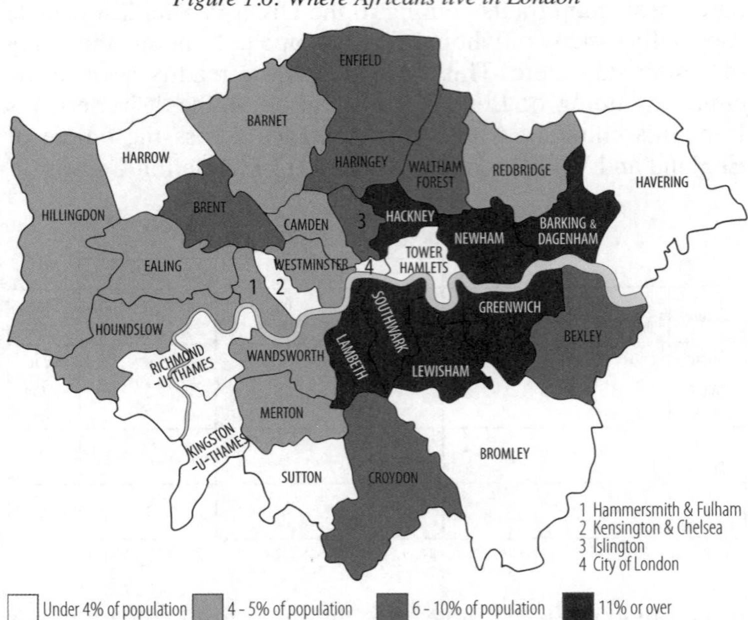

As one might expect, there is a reasonably close correspondence between Figures 1.6 and 1.7 and Figures 1.2 and 1.3, but the correspondence is not total. More than 11% of the population of Barking and Dagenham are Africans, for example, but the number of Pentecostal churches in the Borough is relatively small by comparison with, say, neighbouring Newham. This suggests that lack of a nearby church is not a complete bar to attendance – many are willing to travel on a Sunday, especially as London transport links are reasonably good. Again, between 4 and 6% of the populations of Hillingdon and Hounslow Boroughs are Africans, but the number of Pentecostal churches in those Boroughs is very few, and this implies that some or many churchgoing Africans normally travel to attend church outside their Boroughs.

Figure 1.7: Where Caribbeans live in London

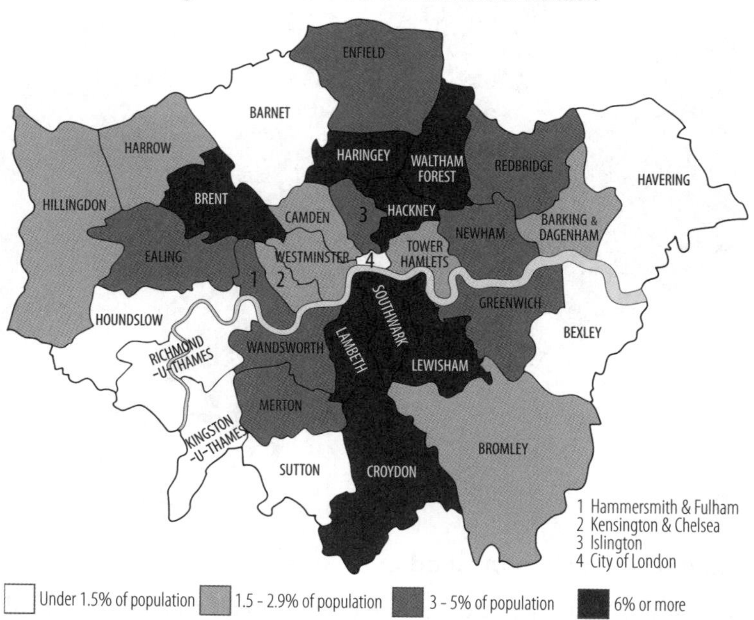

Before we move on to another topic, it is important to realise how exceptional the numbers and distribution of these Pentecostal churches are, as they concentrate in relatively few Boroughs within London, and at the same time, are relatively numerous.

The only other denomination with over a thousand churches in the capital is the Church of England, and Figure 1.8 shows how these are distributed. It should be noted that the bands for the different groups are much narrower than in Figure 1.3 showing the Pentecostal churches, and that the number of Anglican churches is much more uniformly spread across the capital, with the exception perhaps of the City of London, which has 44 churches, but in which less than 0.1% of London's population lives.

Figure 1.8: Distribution of Anglican Churches in London, 2012

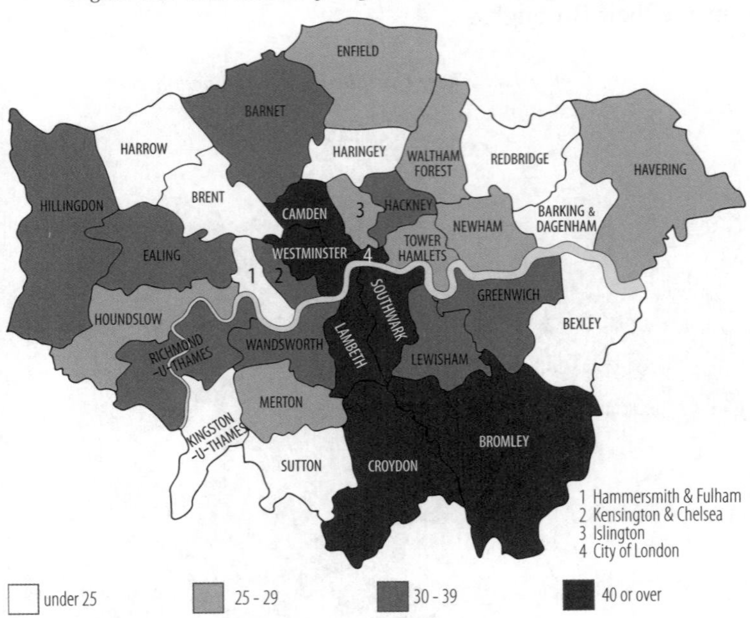

Languages spoken in London's Churches

Immigrant churches are more evenly spread than Pentecostal churches, and may be found across all denominations. There is an Urdu Methodist, a Ghanaian Seventh-Day Adventist, a South African Anglican, a Polish Lutheran, a Chinese United Reformed, two Spanish Baptist churches, even a Roman Catholic Goan church, and so on. Within the capital there are at least 54 different languages!

Some denominations like the Lutherans and the Orthodox have dozens of churches, mostly serving those who have come from different countries within Europe, even if they welcome all nationalities. The Roman Catholics especially have a large number of Chaplaincies serving those from overseas. Likewise, more than 200 of the black churches serve those from Ghana, Nigeria and other African countries, as well as over 400 West Indian churches. Yet there are many whose precise national focus is blurred, welcoming people from anywhere. There are many "International" or "All Nations" churches in London.

Some nationalities have a long history in London. The Chinese and Korean churches, for example, have been in London for several decades, as have Spanish and Portuguese. The Spanish have the largest number of churches, at least 26, followed by 24 Greek (mostly Orthodox), 13 Portuguese, 10 French, 10 Tamil, 9 Italian, 9 Korean, 8 Chinese, 8 Congolese, 8 Ethiopian and 8 German. The Scandinavian countries have also long had Seamen's Missions in London.

Identification of such churches is not easy; it is usually done by the language used in their name, or the specific mention of a particular country; so it is likely a number will have been missed, especially African churches which tend to use a Pentecostal or Bible name rather than a country, such as Rhea, El Shaddai, Aladura or Cherubim and Seraphim.

Table 1.9: Some of the nationalities of London churches

Africaaners	Congolese	Finnish	Indian	Norwegian	Swiss
Albanian	Coptic	French	Iranian	Polish	Syrian
Antiochian	Croatian	German	Irish	Portuguese	Tamil
American	Czech	Ghanaian	Japanese	Romanian	Thai
Armenian	Dutch	Goan	Korean	Russian	Ukrainian
Assyrian	Eritrean	Greek	Latvian	Slovak	Urdu
Brazilian	Estonian	Gujurati	Lithuanian	Spanish	Vietnamese
Byelorussian	Ethiopian	Hungarian	Maltese	Swahili	Zambian
Chinese	Filipino	Icelandic	Nigerian	Swedish	Zimbabwean

Some of the languages spoken are shown in Table 1.9 to illustrate the diversity within London. Many of these churches are evangelical; if an immigrant has to struggle with English from Monday to Saturday, they will often gladly go to a church speaking their language on a Sunday, whether they are used to churchgoing or not, simply to be able to converse in their own tongue! Thus does the Lord build His church despite (or because of) the upheaval of international relocation.

Translation of services

These are churches identifying with a particular nationality. However, in addition, a question not included in previous Censuses, was asked about whether the services were translated into languages other than English. One church in seven, 14%, does so.

Three denominations had very few of their services translated – the Baptists, Independents and United Reformed Church (average 4%). Four denominations had about the average percentage of their services translated – Anglicans, Roman Catholics, Methodists and the New Churches (average 14%). Two denominations had about a quarter (24%) – the Pentecostals and the Smaller denominations – and one denomination all their services – the Orthodox.

Table 1.10: Languages into which London church services were translated

Acholi	Fanti	Hungarian	Mandarin	Serbian	Slovak
(Ugandan)	(Ghana)	Japanese	(Chinese)	Serbo-Croatian	Spanish
Arabic	Filipino	Korean	Persian	Shona	Taiwanese
Assyrian	French	Latin	Portuguese	(Zimbabwe)	Tamil
Cantonese	German	Lingala	Punjabi	Sign language	Xhosa
(Chinese)	Greek	(Congo)	Romanian	(for the deaf)	(South Africa)
Coptic	Gujarati	Lithuanian	Russian	Sinhalese	Yoruba
	Hindustani	Malayalam	Rwandan	(Sri Lanka)	(Nigerian)

An immense variety of languages was used, a selection of which is shown in Table 1.10; to be compared with the nationalities in Table 1.9. A similar range was given when asked the most common nationality in a particular congregation, with proportions using a particular language usually given as a multiple of 5% or 10%. London's churches are multilingual, multinational and multicultural.

Many congregations needing a church ask their local Church of England minister if they can use the parish church, often on an afternoon when there is no Anglican service. Usually, the answer is favourable. An email from the Revd John Chapman, Chaplain for International Churches in the Diocese of London, said:

> I know that in Anglican churches in the London Diocese there are Congolese Congregations in Wembley, Hanwell and Northolt at least; Tamil in Northolt, Southall, South Harrow, Roxeth, Edgware and Alperton; Gujarati in Wembley; Urdu in Southall; Korean in Harrow and Kings Cross; Arabic and Burmese in Ealing; Russian in Ealing and the City; Spanish in Northolt and Muswell Hill; Malayalam in Kings Cross; Brazilian in Hounslow; Chinese in Trafalgar Square; Ethiopians in Cannonbury; Eritreans near Shepherd's Bush; British Orthodox in Shadwell – and many black churches using Anglican churches that are not part of my brief.

Such is London's diversity!

Churchmanship

One other feature is known about London churches other than their denomination and Borough. That is their churchmanship or ethos, obtained from the minister by asking the question, "Which of the following terms best describes your congregation?" A list of 10 words or phrases followed, plus an "Other, please specify" and they were invited to tick up to three. Exactly how these answers were given and then coded into the categories used for Churchmanship is discussed later, but the number of churches in each category is known, albeit not broken down by Inner or Outer London. Details are given in Table 1.11:

Table 1.11: Churchmanship of London Churches, 1989-2020E

	A	B	Ca	Evangelical B	Evangelical M	Evangelical Ch	Evangelical Total	L	LC	O	Total
1989	208	243	582	299	634	785	1,718	442	243	113	3,549
1998	218	202	609	235	932	813	1,980	401	301	153	3,864
2005	232	195	617	239	995	977	2,211	353	303	176	4,087
2012	**238**	**191**	**610**	**222**	**1,191**	**1,492**	**2,905**	**352**	**313**	**182**	**4,791**
2020E	240	189	607	210	1,303	1,653	3,166	330	308	190	5,030
As percentages of Total											
1989 %	*6*	*7*	*16*	*8*	*18*	*22*	*48*	*13*	*7*	*3*	*100*
1998 %	*6*	*5*	*16*	*6*	*24*	*21*	*51*	*10*	*8*	*4*	*100*
2005 %	*6*	*5*	*15*	*6*	*24*	*24*	*54*	*9*	*7*	*4*	*100*
2012 %	***5***	***4***	***13***	***5***	***25***	***31***	***61***	***7***	***6***	***4***	***100***
2020E %	*5*	*4*	*12*	*4*	*26*	*33*	*63*	*6*	*6*	*4*	*100*
Rest of Eng'd 2005	*5*	*14*	*15*	*9*	*17*	*12*	*38*	*12*	*12*	*4*	33,414
All England 2005	*5*	*13*	*15*	*8*	*18*	*14*	*40*	*12*	*11*	*4*	37,501

A=Anglo-Catholic. B=Broad. Ca=Catholic. M=Mainstream. Ch=Charismatic. L=Liberal. LC=Low Church. O=Others. Eng'd=England.

Table 1.11 shows in 2012 three-fifths, 61%, of London's churches were evangelical, against less than two-fifths, 38%, in the rest of England. As evangelical churches are more likely to be growing than non-evangelical churches this may help to explain the huge increase in church numbers – perhaps a greater willingness to plant because the church is more likely to be successful? The percentage of evangelical churches has been increasing for over 20 years and is projected to continue to do so, being 63% by 2020 if present trends continue.

While evangelical churches are increasing in number, Broad or Liberal churches are declining. Anglo-Catholic, Catholic or Low Churches are broadly holding their own or increasing in number. "Catholic" in this context does not just mean "Roman Catholic" as a number of other churches, especially Anglican, will define themselves in this way also.

So what does all this say?

This chapter has looked at the numbers of churches in the capital. The number has grown by about 700 since the previous count in 2005, a rate of 100 per year. Two-thirds of this increase has been due to the growth of black Pentecostal churches, and a third the immigrant churches.

This rate of growth is expected to continue, although at a reduced level, as many of the immigrant churches are now in place. The black Pentecostal churches are likely to carry on growing, however, so that by the year 2020 there could be as many as 5,030 churches in London, an increase of 240 in 8 years, or a rate of increase of 30 a year. The growth has been especially marked in the Boroughs of Enfield, Lambeth, Merton, Newham and Southwark. Large numbers of Pentecostal churches can be seen in the Boroughs of Lambeth, Newham and Southwark. The 2011 Population Census showed high proportions of the populations of these three Boroughs were African, and high proportions of Lambeth and Southwark were Caribbean, indicating the proliferation of churches is among those ethnic groups and close to where they live.

Equally, the Census demographics showed there are other Boroughs where many Africans live (such as Barking & Dagenham and Greenwich) but which do not have numerous Pentecostal churches, while some Boroughs (like Brent and Haringey) have many Pentecostal churches but relatively few Africans, indicating church proximity is not the only factor for growth; travel to a desired congregation is also crucial for many. The number and diversity of immigrant churches is wide, however, and many Anglican churches are used by them. More than 50 nationalities are known to be represented at different churches, and because of the difficulty of identifying the many African churches, the number is almost certainly much higher. One church in seven, 14%, provides a translation service into another language, reflecting the international character of London; a wide variety of languages are used. The Population Census statistics show the huge proportions of non-white people living in London, unlike the rest of England, and future church expansion among these is likely to continue. The issues of language, nationality and church culture are likely to be important in such growth. Finally, the chapter showed a high proportion of London's churches may be classified as Evangelical, much more so than in the rest of England. How far this is directly related to the growth of churches is less clear since "white evangelicalism" and "black evangelicalism" are known to differ on critical parts of biblical hermeneutics, but it is difficult to think there is no relationship since so many of the new churches are black or immigrant.

The number of churches is one thing, and while their statistical analysis may be interesting the numbers who attend them are much more important. Before we look at these, however, it will be worth looking at the Population Census figures on religion, the subject of the next chapter.

2

LONDON'S RELIGIONS FROM THE POPULATION CENSUS

The initial results of the 2011 Population Census about religion were published just before Christmas 2012, and gave the numbers of people who had answered the question "What is your religion?", which gave seven religious choices and a "no religion" box. This question was optional so some people did not answer it. Before we look at the London figures, it may be helpful to briefly look at the national picture, so that the capital's figures can be put into context.

The National Picture

For the country as a whole the answers, with comparative figures from 2001, are shown in Table 2.1[20].

A huge number of people living in Britain were not born here. The Census found that 3.8 million out of the 7.5 million total immigrants in England and Wales arrived between 2001 and 2011. The religion of these incomers will be released by the Office for National Statistics when available, but in a study of immigrants in 2000, it was then found that 31% of immigrants were Christian and 24% Muslim.[21]

As may be seen in Table 2.1, the number of people in England who said they were Muslim increased from 1.5 million in 2001 to 2.7 million in 2011. If the same percentages on religion of immigrants found in the 2000 study hold for those coming between 2001 and 2011, then 0.9 million of these new immigrants were Muslim, a number accounting for the majority of the increase of 1.2 million Muslims between 2001 and 2011.

Table 2.1: Population by Religion, England and Wales, 2001 and 2011

	2001				2011			
	Numbers		Percentages		Numbers		Percentages	
Religion	England	Wales	England %	Wales %	England	Wales	England %	Wales %
Christian	35,251,244	2,087,242	*71.74*	*71.90*	31,479,876	1,763,299	*59.38*	*57.56*
Muslim	1,524,887	21,739	*3.10*	*0.75*	2,660,116	45,950	*5.02*	*1.50*
Hindu	546,982	5,439	*1.11*	*0.19*	806,199	10,434	*1.52*	*0.34*
Sikh	327,343	2,015	*0.67*	*0.07*	420,196	2,962	*0.79*	*0.10*
Jew	257,671	2,256	*0.52*	*0.08*	261,282	2,064	*0.49*	*0.07*
Buddhist	139,046	5,407	*0.28*	*0.18*	238,626	9,117	*0.45*	*0.30*
Other religions	143,811	6,909	*0.29*	*0.24*	227,825	12,705	*0.43*	*0.41*
No Religion	7,171,332	537,935	*14.60*	*18.53*	13,114,232	982,997	*24.74*	*32.09*
Not stated	3,776,515	234,143	*7.69*	*8.06*	3,804,104	233,928	*7.18*	*7.63*
TOTAL	49,138,831	2,903,085	*100*	*100*	53,012,456	3,063,456	*100*	*100*

Of all the different religions in the UK, the rate of change between 2001 and 2011 is greatest amongst Muslims, and in Wales their number has more than doubled, as may be seen in Table 2.2. In his book *Slippery Slope: The Islamisation of the UK,* Patrick Sookhdeo, General Director of the Barnabasfund, warns of the increasing numbers. He launched "Operation Nehemiah" in February 2011 to alert political and senior church leaders of this. Numbers from the 2011 Census show Muslims are already almost at the level previously predicted for 2020.

While Muslims are 5% of the English population (and 1½% of the Welsh), all the other religions together amount to just over 3% in England (and just over 1% in Wales). The Census category "Other religions" is a summation of many groups, the largest of which (England and Wales together) is Pagan, with 57,000 people. This is followed by 53,000 Spiritual/Spiritualists, 24,000 "Mixed religion," 20,000 Jains, 12,000 associating with Wicca, 11,000 Ravidassians, 8,000 Rastafarians, 5,000 Baha'is, 4,000 Druids, 4,000 Taoists, and 4,000 Zoroastrians, with over 30 other smaller categories.

Table 2.2: Percentage change in number of adherents 2001 to 2011

% Change	Christian %	Buddhist %	Hindu %	Jew %	Muslim %	Sikh %	Other %	No Rel %	Not ans. %	Overall %
England	-11	72	47	1	74	28	58	83	1	8
Wales	-16	69	92	-9	111	47	84	83	0	6

The group "No religion" includes 177,000 Jedi Knights (a designation by the Office for National Statistics), 32,000 Agnostics, 29,000 Atheists, 15,000 Humanists, 6,000 Heavy Metal followers, 500 Free Thinkers and 350 "Realists."

In general, Christianity in Wales has declined slightly more than in England, and other religions, especially Islam, have increased faster (except for the Buddhists and Jews). There were many more, pro rata, who said they had no religion in Wales than in England (32% to 25%), but the proportion following other religions is much smaller than in England (3% to 9%).

The Christian Total

The number of people calling themselves Christian in England alone declined from 35.3 million in 2001 to 31.5 million in 2011, a drop of 3.8 million, and, as a percentage of the population, a decline from 72% to 59%. In Wales it dropped from 2.1 million to 1.8 million, and from 72% to 58% of the population.

Many commentators seem to assume these declines reflect a falling away of belief in a secular age, and, while that is bound to be part of the explanation, it may not be the main reason. The Church of England Research Department annually collects data on funerals. In the 10 years between 2001 and 2011, its ministers conducted 2.2 million funerals, roughly half (49%) church funerals and half (51%) crematoria funerals.[22] It is perhaps reasonable to assume those wishing to have an Anglican minister conducting their funeral would probably have ticked "Christian" on their Census form had they been alive at the time of the Census. In the same period there have been 4.8 million deaths in England, so Church of England clergy have presided at almost half (46%) of the country's funerals.

Few other denominations publish the number of funerals taken by their clergy or deaths of their members. The Roman Catholic Church, however, is one which does, and in this 10-year period 0.4 million Roman Catholics died, and, again, one presumes that all these would have said they were Christian (irrespective of whether they regularly attended Mass) had they been alive to tick the Census form. The Methodist Church has also collected the same information from 2007, and grossing up their deaths for a 10-year period is a further 0.2 million.

In membership terms, Anglicans, Roman Catholics and Methodists accounted for 62% of (alive) church members in England in 2010. Were the death rate in other denominations to be similar to that of these three, then if 2.2 + 0.4 + 0.2 = 2.8 million deaths represent 62% of church membership, total church deaths in the Census decade could have been some 4.5 million people, much greater than the actual drop in Christian adherents recorded by the Census. However, the actual number is likely to be somewhat less, say 4.3 million Christian deaths (representing 90% of all those who died in the decade), as some denominations, like the Pentecostals, are much younger and have fewer deaths.

Those joining

Offsetting the decline in the number of Christians is the number who have joined the church in this period. This is more difficult to evaluate but in the period 1998 to 2005 it was estimated (in my book *Pulling out of the Nosedive*) that 850,000 people joined the church in England. That rate of joining over those seven years might not be as great in the period 2005 to 2011, so that perhaps between 2001 and 2011, say, a million people (rather than 1.2 million which is the pro rata figure) joined the church. The overall equation then becomes, in millions:

> + 1.0 who joined – 4.3 who died – 0.5 other leavers = – 3.8 decrease.

If this equation is approximately true, it demonstrates that the large bulk of the decline in the number of Christians between 2001 and 2011 is because of the number who died, rather than a dropping away for other reasons. The equation also explains the catastrophic forecast given at the Church of England July 2012 Synod that their attendance is expected to decline by almost 60% by 2030, since the number joining the C of E is so very much smaller than the large number who are dying. It also puts the church's evangelistic work into context, and highlights the enormous urgency to increase it, in fact, to quadruplicate or even quintuplicate it.

In 2005, 35% of Anglicans were 65 or over. The proportion of Baptists 65 or over was 25%, lower than the Church of England, and thus fewer Baptist deaths pro rata can be expected in the days ahead. However, it is still likely that people joining the Baptist churches will be fewer than the number dying, so a decline in the number of Baptists will occur, unless action can be taken to change the situation. Baptist attendance in England declined 8% between 1998 and 2005.

What is "Christian"?

In a very helpful article about the Census results, Linda Woodhead, Professor of Sociology of Religion at Lancaster University, suggests the simple range of answers to the Census question does not really indicate religious identity.[23] She refers to recent publications which break down the "Christian" category into:

- Moral Christians, who admire Christian ethics and aspire to live by them.
- Faithful Christians, who do orthodox things such as attending church and reading the Bible.
- Cradle Christians, who tick the box because they were baptised and brought up Christian.
- Ethnic Christians who say they are Christian because they are British.

Furthermore, research has found that at least 12% of Census Christians do not consider themselves religious, only 54%

believe in a personal God, and, according to latest attendance figures, 90% do not attend church.

No religion

In the study of immigrants in 2000, 21% said they had no religion which, if true of the 3.8 million coming in the inter-Census period, would mean some 12% of the increase in those saying they have "No religion" in the 2011 Census would be simply due to new immigrants in our midst.[24] Almost certainly, many of those saying they had no religion in 2011 would be young people, some of whom in a previous generation would have joined the church. Again the scale of the loss of young people to the church is put into some sort of perspective.

Linda Woodhead quotes Theos think-tank surveys to indicate that "No religion" does not necessarily mean secular. In fact, Theos research suggests No-religionists divide into three categories – the non-attenders, the atheists and the non-religious. However, 44% of the non-attenders believe in a soul and 35% in God or a higher power, 23% of atheists believe in a soul, and 34% of the non-religious believe in life after death and 10% that God designed the world. In other words, many of those indicating "No religion" in the 2011 Census mean they have no formal adherence to any religious body, though they may have certain religious beliefs of their own.

Some of those ticking "No religion", as well as some of those not answering the question at all, might still say they were "spiritual", even if the meaning of such is indeterminate, since other research has shown that more people identify themselves as "spiritual" rather than "religious." The increase seen in "No religion" might suggest a more secular population, but only because "secular", "spiritual" and "religion" lack any clear definition.

The London Scene: All Religions

The basic numbers given by respective Censuses for those following different religions in Greater London are given in

Table 2.3, with the national percentages repeated from Table 2.1 for comparison.

Table 2.3: Population by Religion, Greater London, 2001 and 2011

Religion	2001			2011		
	Numbers in London	Percentages		Numbers in London	Percentages	
		London	England		London	England
Christian	4,176,175	*58.23*	*71.74*	3,957,984	*48.42*	*59.38*
Muslim	607,083	*8.47*	*3.10*	1,012,823	*12.39*	*5.02*
Hindu	291,977	*4.07*	*1.11*	411,291	*5.03*	*1.52*
Sikh	104,230	*1.45*	*0.67*	126,134	*1.54*	*0.79*
Jew	149,789	*2.09*	*0.52*	148,602	*1.82*	*0.49*
Buddhist	54,297	*0.76*	*0.28*	82,026	*1.00*	*0.45*
Other religions	36,558	*0.51*	*0.29*	47,970	*0.59*	*0.43*
No Religion	1,130,616	*15.76*	*14.60*	1,694,372	*20.73*	*24.74*
Not stated	621,366	*8.66*	*7.69*	692,739	*8.48*	*7.18*
TOTAL	7,172,091	*100*	*100*	8,173,941	*100*	*100*
Total as % of England		*14.60*	~		*15.42*	~

It is evident from Table 2.3 that the religious composition of the population of London contrasts strongly with England as a whole. In 2011, less than half (48%) would define themselves as Christian and only just over a fifth (21%) would say they had no religion, percentages comparing respectively with 59% and 25% for the country as a whole. Fewer "no-religionists" in London, and a smaller proportion of Christians reflect the much greater numbers of those belonging to other religions in the capital.

Changes over the 10-year inter-Censal period

The religion which has grown most in the ten inter-Censal years is Islam, up from 8% of London's population in 2001 to 12% in 2011. Table 2.4 shows how each religion has changed in this period.

Table 2.4: Percentage change in number of adherents 2001 to 2011

% Change	Christian %	Buddhist %	Hindu %	Jew %	Muslim %	Sikh %	Other %	No Rel %	Not ans. %	Overall %
London	-5	51	41	-1	67	21	31	50	11	14
England	-11	72	47	1	74	28	58	83	1	8

While the changes in Table 2.4 seem quite severe, when set alongside the changes as a whole in England they are comparable, except that the percentage who didn't answer the religion question at all is much higher. The Christian numbers in London have not reduced pro rata as much as in England as a whole.

If one ignores the "not answered", then the 2011 Census results show of the population of London, half (53%) are adherents to Christianity, a quarter (23%) have no religion, one in seven (13%) are Muslim, and the remaining ninth (11%) belong to other religions.

Detail by Borough

The Census figures broken down by Borough are also available, and the detail is given in *Church Statistics*. They show (all the percentages being the percentage of the Borough population):

- **Inner London** is less Christian than Outer London (45% to 50%), but more non-religious (24% to 19%) and more Muslim (14% to 11%).
- The **least Christian** Boroughs are Tower Hamlets (27%), Camden (34%), Redbridge (37%) and Hackney (39%).
- The **most Christian** Boroughs are Havering (66%), Bexley (62%) and Bromley (61%). In Inner London, the most Christian Boroughs are Hammersmith & Fulham and Kensington & Chelsea (both 54%).
- **Hindus** are strongest in Harrow (25%), Brent (18%), Redbridge (11%) and Hounslow (10%).
- **Muslims** are especially strong in Tower Hamlets (35%) and Newham (32%), followed by Redbridge (23%) and Waltham Forest (22%). They are weakest in Bexley, Bromley (2½% each) and Havering (2%).

- **Jews** are strongest in Barnet (15%), Hackney (6%) and Camden (5%).
- **Sikhs** are strongest in Hounslow (9%), Ealing (8%), Hillingdon (7%) and Redbridge (6%).
- **Other religions** are strongest in Harrow (2½%), Brent and Barnet (1% each), and **Buddhists** are fairly uniform at about 1% everywhere.
- Those with **no religion** are strongest in the City of London (34%), Islington (30%), and Hackney, Lambeth and Richmond upon Thames (all 28%), and weakest in Harrow and Newham (10% each).
- The **overall population** grew most in Tower Hamlets in the inter-censal period (up 30%) and Newham (up 26%), and least in the City of London (up 3%) and Kensington & Chelsea (where it stayed the same).

The distribution of Christians and Muslims is probably the most important element of the 2011 Census for the purposes of this book, and this is shown in the maps in Figures 2.6 and 2.7:

Figure 2.6: Where Christians live in London

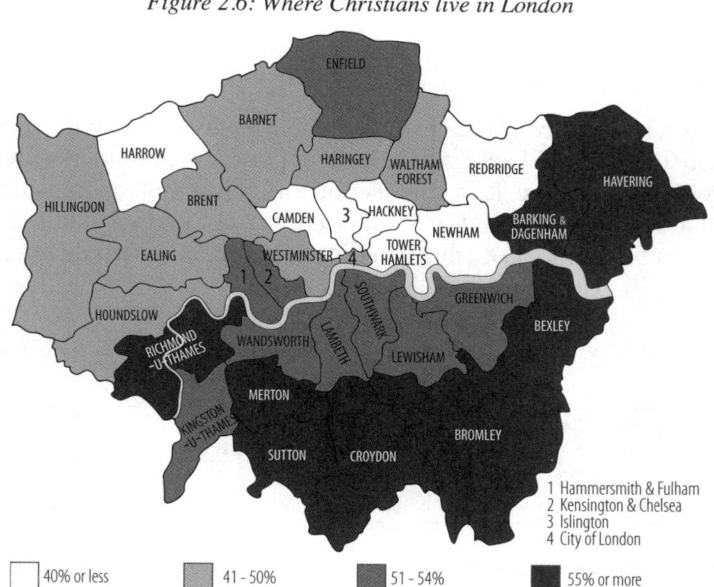

Figure 2.7: Where Muslims live in London

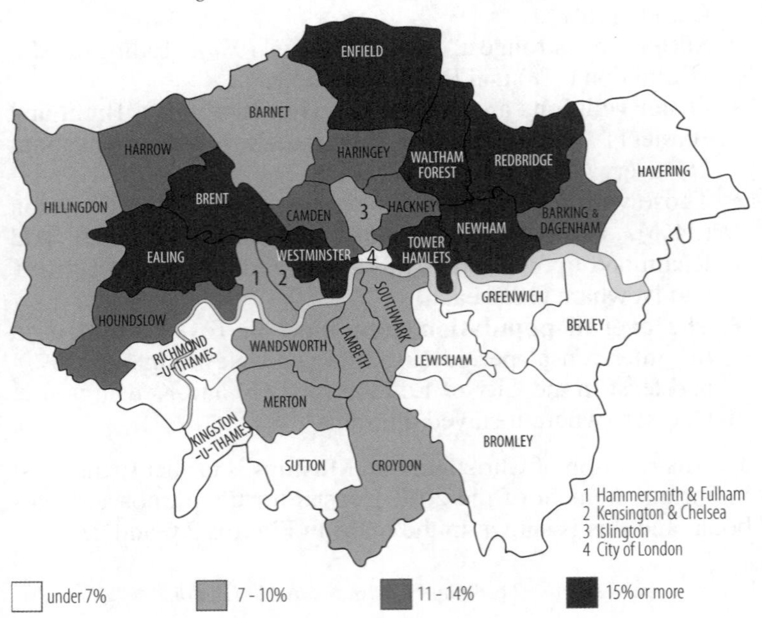

Travel in London

It is clear many travel to church in London. The published statistics on travel unfortunately do not break the numbers down by days of the week, so the use of different kinds of transport on a Sunday compared with other days is not known. Table 2.8 shows the number of trips taken by Londoners in two different years, 10 years apart.[25]

Table 2.8: Percentage of trips taken in London by different modes, 1999 and 2009

Mode of travel	Rail %	Under-ground %	Bus %	Taxi %	Car driver %	Car pas-senger %	Motor cycle %	Cycle %	Walk %	Base (=100%)
1999	*7*	*8*	*11*	*1*	*31*	*16*	*1*	*1*	*24*	22.4 m
2009	*9*	*9*	*14*	*1*	*26*	*14*	*1*	*2*	*24*	24.4 m

It may be seen trips by public transport (rail, underground and bus) have increased in this period (26% to 32%), while trips by car have decreased (48% to 41%). This increase is probably due to a combination of congestion charges, parking problems, rising cost of fuel, cycling schemes, encouragement to use public transport, and, perhaps, very marginally, more people travelling to attend church!

While the number of cars actually owned by Londoners increased by 8% between 2001 and 2011, the actual number of cars owned per person dropped slightly from 0.87 per person to 0.82. This compares with an 8% increase in car ownership across England as a whole, with the average number owned per person increasing slightly from 1.11 to 1.17.[26] This fall in ownership in London presumably corresponds to the smaller number of trips taken by car in the capital.

The 1851 Census

The previous paragraphs have looked at the results from the 2001 and 2011 Population Censusses. However, there was another Population Census which asked questions about religion – in 1851. It is said, when the results became known, that Parliament decided not to include such questions in any future Census as they did not wish to know "Dissenters" (that is, non-Anglicans) were in a majority![27] That decision was overturned 150 years later.

In 1851, most churches had two or even three services on a Sunday. The Census counted the number of attenders at each service, but made no attempt to ascertain how many separate individuals were in attendance. The population of England and Wales, as measured, was 17,927,609, and 25% attended public worship on the morning of 30 March 1851, 17% in the afternoon, and 16% in the evening. No-one assumes these were all different people, so the total of 58% has to be reduced, and different authorities make different assumptions. An analysis in the book *The Tide is Running Out* assumed those going at least once was 24%,[28] presuming the same proportion going more than once as was ascertained in another study in 1903 (meaning a large proportion of these went twice and a substantial proportion all three times).

A total of 33,913 churches were counted in England and Wales (43,700 in 2010), of which 13,000 (38%) had been built before 1801, and respectively 4%, 6%, 9%, 14% and 16% were built in each of the following 5 decades (with the building date of 13% not recorded), showing an increasing number of new churches were started as the Industrial Revolution, and its large-scale movement of people for employment, got under way (building churches near to where people then lived). In 1851, 3% of the country's total churches were in London, by 2012, 11% were, showing the growth of London in these 160 years.

The denominations of the 1851 churches differed greatly from those in 2012, especially as the New Churches and Pentecostals had not begun in 1851. London was not then a unified area but consisted of eight Municipal/Parliamentary Boroughs, shown in detail in Table 2.9. Smaller Denominations were then principally the Society of Friends, Lady of Huntingdon's Connexion and a few Lutheran churches. Within "Independents" were seven London City Mission churches. The 1851 Census also listed some 222 Mormon, 229 Unitarian and 50 Swedenborgian New Churches and 53 Jewish synagogues as the only other places of worship. Table 2.10 gives a comparison and includes the 1903 figures also given in the next section (the 2012 numbers come from Table 1.4):

Table 2.9: Churches in London by Parliamentary Borough, by current denomination, 1851

Parliamentary Borough 1851	Anglican	Baptist	Roman Catholic	Independent	Methodist	New	Orthodox	Pentecostal	Presbyterian	Smaller Denoms	Total
Finsbury	46	20	5	31	16	0	0	0	3	1	122
Greenwich	21	11	3	14	15	0	0	0	3	1	68
Lambeth	36	13	1	20	21	0	0	0	0	2	93
City of London	73	4	2	13	4	0	1	0	4	7	108
Marylebone	55	13	8	22	16	0	1	0	3	2	120
Southwark	32	15	3	14	13	0	0	0	1	1	79
Tower Hamlets	65	30	7	61	34	0	0	0	2	7	206
Westminster	59	4	5	11	9	0	0	0	4	5	97
Total	387	110	34	186	128	0	2	0	20	26	893

Table 2.10: Percentage of churches in London by denomination, 1851 and 2012

Denomination	Anglican %	Baptist %	Roman Catholic %	Independent %	Methodist %	New %	Orthodox %	Pentecostal %	Presbyterian %	Smaller Denoms %	Base =100%
1851	*44*	*12*	*4*	*21*	*14*	*0*	*0.2*	*0*	*2*	*3*	893
1903	*38*	*11*	*4*	*16*	*12*	*0*	*0.1*	*0*	*3*	*16*	3,911
2012	*21*	*8*	*8*	*7*	*5*	*6*	*2*	*30*	*3*	*10*	4,791

The 1886 Survey

In 1886 a Census of all London churches was undertaken by Dr Robertson Nicoll, and the results published in the first issues of the *British Weekly* journal. He sought to count attendance by personally observing and recording the number of worshippers going into a church for the main Sunday morning service (invariably at 11 am) and the evening service, using a number of enumerators. This was done without differentiating numbers by age or gender, and excluded earlier services. The total attendance was estimated at 1,167,000, or 31% of the then population of 3,816,000.

The 1903 London Census

In 1903 Richard Mudie-Smith attempted to improve these results by again personally counting the worshippers as they entered a church on a Sunday, but this time including every service, and seeking to observe all the churches in London, one or two Boroughs at a time, across a whole year of observation (November 1902 to November 1903) using paid enumerators.[29] The results were published in *The Daily News*. He also counted those who attended twice, and excluded them as his interest was in the number of attenders. The year 1903 happened to be exceptionally wet, but he concluded a rainy Sunday did not adversely affect church attendance.

At that time London consisted of 29 Boroughs and had a total population of 4,537,000, of whom 22% were counted attending church (when the 66,000 living in institutions were excluded), which included some twicers, and 19% attending just once. Two-fifths, 43%, of these were Church of England, 43% other denominations, 8% Roman Catholic and 6% designated "other services". The population had clearly risen quite sharply in the intervening period and the number of worshippers had dropped – by about 150,000, virtually all of whom were Church of England.

The 29 "London" Boroughs were surrounded by 52 Districts, which together with the Boroughs, made up "Greater London". These were the pre-cursors to what is now called Inner London (the Boroughs, grouped together from 29 into 14) and Outer London (the 52 Districts now grouped into 19 Boroughs). Church attendance was measured in both, and the detail, by morning and evening attendance, is given in Table 2.11:

Table 2.11: Morning and evening church attendance, London, 1903

Time of day	Inner London				Outer London				All London			
	Men %	Women %	Children %	Total %	Men %	Women %	Children %	Total %	Men %	Women %	Children %	Total %
Morning	*14*	*18*	*18*	*50*	*12*	*16*	*19*	*47*	*13*	*18*	*18*	*49*
Evening	*13*	*23*	*14*	*50*	*14*	*26*	*13*	*53*	*13*	*24*	*14*	*51*
Overall	*27*	*41*	*32*	*100*	*26*	*42*	*32*	*100*	*26*	*42*	*32*	*100*
Base =100%	266,600	413,000	323,700	1,003,300	132,500	215,200	163,000	510,700	399,100	628,200	486,700	1,514,000

In 1903, Inner London accounted for two-thirds, 66%, of total London church attendance, against 44% in 2012, a century later. The gender of the children was not noted in 1903, but of the adults, men were two-fifths, 38%, of the total, against 42% of adults in 2012. Virtually as many went to church in the morning as the evening, though with slightly more evening worshippers in Outer London. Children were a third, 32%, of all attenders, against a fifth, 21%, in 2012; part of the reason for the change is that adults were living 30 years longer on average in 2012 (life expectancy was 51 in 1911 and 81 in 2011[30]).

In terms of denomination, Roman Catholics were a little stronger in Inner London than Outer (10% to 6%), and Methodists stronger in Outer than Inner (13% to 10%) but otherwise there was little variation in the denominational spread.

Table 2.12: Sunday church attendance by denomination in London, 1903 and 2012

Denomination	Anglican %	Baptist %	R Cath. %	Indep. %	Meth. %	New %	Ortho. %	Pente. %	Pres. %	Smaller %	Total %
1903 % of total	*44*	*11*	*8*	*14*	*12*	*0*	*0*	*0*	*3*	*8*	*100*
2012 % of total	*12*	*6*	*27*	*4*	*2*	*6*	*3*	*32*	*1*	*7*	*100*

However, the above scene is in sharp contrast to the picture today, as shown in Table 2.12. The Anglican proportion has decreased substantially, and the Roman Catholic and Pentecostal proportions increased; the Pentecostals did not begin as a movement until 1906.

In 1903 there were 3,911 churches in London; two-thirds, 67%, in Inner London. The average attendance was 385 per church (including twicers). A breakdown of them by denomination is given in Table 2.10, and excludes 30 Unitarian, 12 New Jerusalem and 8 Christadelphian churches, as well as 65 Jewish synagogues. Smaller denominations included 11% of churches simply labelled "Other services"; they included 150 Salvation Army churches.

So what does all this say?

The 2011 Population Census revealed a drop in the number of people calling themselves Christian in England and Wales, while adherents of other religions generally rose. The two which rose fastest were the Muslims (now 5% of England's population) and the Buddhists (only ½%).

The Christian decline is largely due to the number of elderly Christian people dying. An estimated 4.3 million people who would have ticked "Christian" on the Census form died between 2001 and 2011 in England, and another 0.5 million stopped being "Christians" for various reasons, but these were somewhat offset by 1.0 million people who joined or re-joined the church, giving the overall drop of 3.8 million or 11% of the 2011 numbers. "Christian" in this context is a term meaning different things to different people.

In London the decline in adherents to Christianity was much smaller – just 5%, and London "Christians" now represent an eighth, 13%, of all the Christians in England, a marginal increase on the 12% in 2001. On the other hand, while other religions in London also increased in numbers, they did so less in percentage terms than the rest of the country. This means London is slightly more "Christian", in Census terms, than elsewhere in England, but it had a marginally higher percentage of people who did not answer the Census religion question (8%

to 7%).

Christians are by no means uniformly distributed across London. There is a distinct "Bible belt" in the Eastern and Southern Boroughs, stretching from Havering in the east through Bexley and Bromley in the south-east on to Richmond upon Thames in the south-west. More than a quarter, 28%, of London's Christians live in these eight Boroughs, against 23% of the total population.

On the other hand, there is a distinct sparsity of Christians in seven Boroughs immediately north of the Thames in central London (Camden, Hackney, Islington, Newham, Redbridge and Tower Hamlets, and also Harrow). In these Boroughs just 16% of the capital's Christians live, against 21% of the population as a whole.

A similar concentration is true of Muslims. They are largely absent in Boroughs where Christians are strong, and much more present in Boroughs where Christians are weak. While Muslims are 12% of London's population as a whole, they are 22% or more of the population in the eight Boroughs where they are strongest (Brent, Ealing, Enfield, Newham, Redbridge, Tower Hamlets, Waltham Forest and Westminster), and in these Boroughs more than half, 51%, of all London's Muslims live.

Other religions also have Boroughs in which they are especially strong – Hindus in Harrow (25% of the population), Jews in Barnet (15%), Sikhs in Hounslow (9%), and Other Religions in Harrow (3%), though the Buddhists are not concentrated in any particular area.

More use is being made of public transport now in London (32% of all trips), and private car is used less (40%), while walking still accounts for a quarter (24%) of journeys. This will include some of those travelling to church on a Sunday and other activities on weekdays.

In 1851, the Census showed far fewer churches in London

pro rata, just 3% of the total, against 11% today. Of that 3% almost half were Church of England and a fifth were Methodist. These numbers help put into perspective the huge Pentecostal revolution yet to begin, which has added so many churches in the last few years. In the 128 years between 1851 and 1979, 2,500 churches were started in London, and nearly 1,500 in the 33 years between 1979 and 2012, more than double the average annual number of the earlier period.

We have set the scene of where church buildings and Christians are located. Now, we must answer the question, "How many actually go to church?"

3

Churchgoing in London

The number of people attending church on a typical Sunday in London has increased from the time it was last measured in 2005. Then it was 623,000; in 2012 it has increased by almost 100,000 people, to 721,000. That is a considerable increase, almost offsetting the national decline in churchgoing outside London in the same period. So, because of London's increase, national church attendance in England remained virtually static (instead of declining) between 2010 and 2012![31] This remarkable impact is because London's church attendance in 2012 is about a quarter (24%) of that of the whole country. The change can be seen in Figure 3.1, but note the time intervals around the year 2012 are not five years as in the rest of the chart.

Figure 3.1: Church attendance in Greater London and the rest of England, 1990 to 2020E

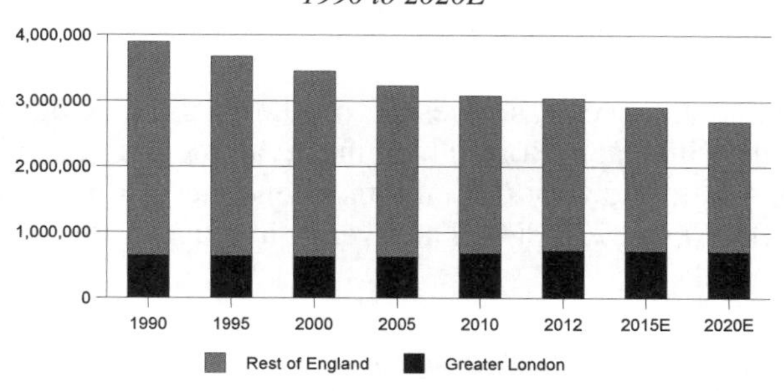

Unfortunately, the overall trend continues downwards, and the increase seen between 2005 and 2012 in London is not expected to continue. The number of people attending church in Greater London is likely to fall slightly in the immediate future, dropping to perhaps 704,000 by 2020. The reasons for this are important, and are explained below.

Calculating overall London attendance

Calculating the total church attendance in Greater London is a complicated affair, worth detailing in order to prove its robustness. Records of church attendance were available for over 54% of the capital's churches, with a large enough direct response to be statistically viable (see note 13).

The average size of a church from these responses multiplied by the number of churches gave one estimate. How could one be sure the responding churches were a representative sample of all churches in London? The average size was 151 people, when the average in 2005 was 152, in 1998 was 160 and in 1989 was 183. In 2005 18% of churches were between 26 and 50 people, and 27% were between 51 and 100 people; the 2012 census gave similar percentages of 18% and 26% respectively, sufficiently comparable to ensure the overall average was reasonable.

It was also possible to break the figures down by denomination. Naturally, some denominations have larger congregations than others, but the average size for all except the Roman Catholics proved similar to previous figures. Past figures were also projected to give estimates. A similar procedure was followed with regard to churchmanship.

Finally, attendance was assessed on the basis of geographical location, with each Borough being evaluated. Each of these methods yielded a very similar total attendance estimate ranging from 706,000 to 729,000. The overall average of these figures was then taken.

Increased number of attenders

It is not surprising that the number of people going to church in London has increased, given that an extra 700 churches have started in the capital in the last few years. In 2005 the total was 623,000 people; in 2012 it was 721,500 people, an increase of 16%. However, the number of churches rose from 4,087 in

2005 to 4,791 in 2012, an increase of 17%. In other words, the increased attendance did not quite keep pace with the formation of new churches, meaning the new churches were, on average, smaller than the existing churches. This is not unusual as it takes time for new churches to grow their congregation. As already noted, the average size was slightly smaller in 2012 which is consistent with this.

It would seem there are three trends contributing to this total:

- There are the new churches, largely BMCs and Immigrant churches which perhaps draw mainly on new people settling in the city and are only marginally touching, or reaching out, to the existing population. The total contribution of these new churches to the total in London is estimated at 24%, a quarter of all churchgoers.
- There are a significant number of larger churches in London, and this proportion has increased. Across England as a whole 11% of churches have congregations in excess of 200 people. In London, in 2005, 21% had congregations of this size, virtually double the national average, and in 2012 the percentage was similar, 23%. The combined congregations of these large churches is over half (54%) of the number of total London churchgoers.
- There remain a sizeable number of churches, 50% or half of all the churches in London, whose combined congregations form just a fifth, 22%, of the capital's churchgoers. These churches overall are reducing in size. For example, 10% of London's churches had congregations of 25 or fewer in 2005; in 2012 that percentage had increased to 12%.

So, while the overall average size of a London church may be twice the average size of a church in England, in reality, the relatively large number of big churches – some of which have very large congregations (some of the largest in the country) – distorts the overall picture. Take these out, and London is a collection of many small churches, more than half of which have congregations of under 100 people. Just over 100 churches in London have a Sunday congregation in single figures. So the existence of many small churches, whose attendance collectively is declining is why the long term future of London's church attenders is likely to decrease rather than increase. These three groups are illustrated in Figure 3.2.

Figure 3.2: Churches and their attenders by group in London, 2012

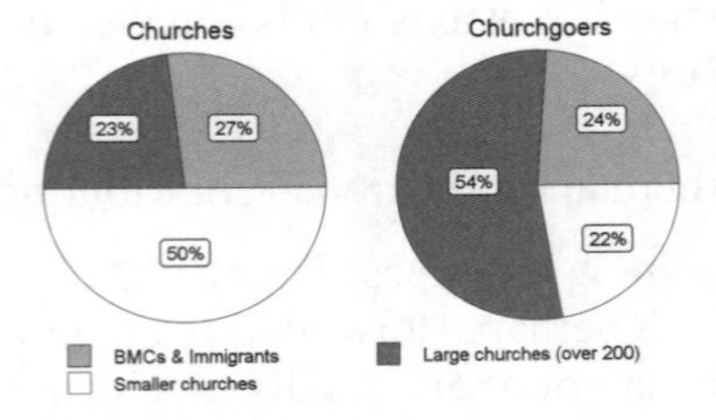

Attendance by Denomination

Table 3.3 gives the Sunday attendance in London for each denomination from past Censuses, and their proportion of the total London attendance, for each of the years it was measured between 1979 and 2005, the latest figures for 2012 and an extrapolation to 2020.

It can be seen that the overall numbers attending church in Greater London declined between 1979 and 1998, and predictions for the future based on this data presumed decline would continue.[32] The impact of the migration beginning especially in the late 1990s and early 2000s was not appreciated until the 2005 Census, which showed an increase in Greater London.

The *Anglicans* are declining in their proportion of the total in London, but at a much slower rate than in the rest of the country where they are forecast to reduce 23% between 2012 and 2020.[33] The likely decline in London is only a third of that, 7%. Part of the reason is that there are some very large Anglican churches in the capital (such as Holy Trinity, Brompton, All Souls, Langham Place, St Helen's, Bishopsgate in Inner London and several others in Outer London), which are unlikely to decline in the next few years. However, almost three-fifths (58%) of Anglican churches in London have congregations under 100, and, collectively, these are likely to decline.

Table 3.3: Denominational attendance and percentage of the total, London, 1979-2020E

Denomination	Anglican	Baptist	Roman Catholic	Independent	Methodist	New	Orthodox	Pentecostal	URC	Smaller Denoms	Total
1979	140,500	46,600	333,700	29,800	35,000	8,100	5,300	57,500	19,600	19,900	696,000
1989	98,500	41,100	293,000	40,900	25,900	26,500	6,400	82,700	16,400	18,200	649,600
1998	101,100	45,800	237,200	24,700	23,700	34,600	16,400	93,700	16,600	24,100	617,900
2005	90,300	46,200	195,400	29,800	20,600	39,700	16,600	152,700	9,300	22,400	623,000
% change 05-12	*-6%*	*-9%*	*+1%*	*-1%*	*-11%*	*+15%*	*+20%*	*+50%*	*-14%*	*+117%*	*+16%*
2012	**84,800**	**41,900**	**198,300**	**29,500**	**18,300**	**43,200**	**19,900**	**229,000**	**8,000**	**48,600**	**721,500**
2020E	78,800	43,000	193,800	29,600	15,200	44,500	21,600	237,100	6,500	34,000	704,100
1979 % of total	*20*	*7*	*48*	*4*	*5*	*1*	*1*	*8*	*3*	*3*	*100*
1989 % of total	*15*	*6*	*45*	*6*	*4*	*4*	*1*	*13*	*3*	*3*	*100*
1998 % of total	*16*	*7*	*38*	*4*	*4*	*6*	*3*	*15*	*3*	*4*	*100*
2005 % of total	*15*	*7*	*31*	*5*	*3*	*6*	*3*	*24*	*2*	*4*	*100*
2012 % of total	***12***	***6***	***27***	***4***	***2***	***6***	***3***	***32***	***1***	***7***	***100***
2020E % of total	*11*	*6*	*28*	*4*	*2*	*6*	*3*	*34*	*1*	*5*	*100*

Baptists in London have seen their numbers remain broadly about 40 to 45,000 over the past 30 years, with a few new churches starting and a few closing (Table 1.4). Essentially, in London they are holding their own, but, as in England generally, they are a "denomination of small churches" with just 25 churches with a congregation of over 200.

The *Roman Catholics* have seen a slight increase in their numbers since 2005, largely because of immigration from European Catholic countries, especially Poland. Polish is now the most common language spoken in Britain after English, but the Poles have dispersed throughout the country, so their impact on London is relatively small. Furthermore, the Roman Catholics are following a policy of closing some of their smaller churches, merging congregations together. Unlike when the Methodists did this in Cornwall in the 1980s, this does not seem to have had a disastrous effect on congregations, perhaps because travel in London on a Sunday is relatively easy. The Catholics have a significant number of large churches in London and some of these, especially those with over a 1,000 attending Sunday Mass, have seen their numbers drop.

The *Independent* churches are made up of various groups. The Congregational churches are few, and generally fairly small. The Christian Brethren are more numerous, with about 100 meeting places, Assemblies or Gospel Halls, and several have congregations in three figures; few of these have closed in the last few years, although more may do so in the future. The majority of the Independent churches are just that, although a fifth are linked to the Fellowship of Independent Evangelical Churches. One very sizeable church is Westminster Chapel, a church of more than 600, and growing, and another is the Metropolitan Tabernacle (whose minister, Dr Peter Masters, starting there in 1970, is one of the longest serving in the country). There are other substantial churches also, such as Enfield Evangelical Free Church with a congregation of over 400, or other Evangelical (Free) Churches (EFC) or Christian Centres, often combined with the name of a town or area, such as Romford EFC or The Slade EC, in Plumstead. However, the largest Independent church of all is Hillsong with some 6,000 in attendance. Apart from a boost in the 1980s, the Independent churches collectively have remained at abo ut 30,000 in London, and look set to do the same over the next eight years; smaller congregations being offset by the launch of further churches (some 50 more are expected, Table 1.4). Some of the Independent churches are better known as "emerging churches", "messy churches" or "fresh expressions", although some of these are part of a specific denominational group also. A proportion of the churches likely to open between 2012 and 2020 will be this type of church. Pro rata, there are rather fewer Independent churchgoers in London than in England as a whole (4% to 6%).

The *Methodists* have been in continuous decline in London since

1979 and are likely to see the same between now and 2020. The Methodists have few large churches, in London or elsewhere, and more than five out of every six has a congregation of under 100. This makes it difficult for very small churches to survive, even with a shared Circuit minister. Even so, in London they are declining less quickly than elsewhere and their 200 plus churches are a witness throughout the capital. However, they are less represented in London than elsewhere – 2% of London's congregations as against 9% in England as a whole. They have seen their congregations almost halve – from 138, on average, in 1979 to 75 in 2012.

New Churches or House Churches have on the whole decentralised from the many streams into which they were grouped in the 1990s and are almost indistinguishable from Independent churches apart from their background. They grew in London, as in the rest of England, in the 1980s, a growth which slowed in the 1990s, but is still likely to continue, though even more slowly. Like the Baptists, they form 6% of London's churchgoers, about the same as in the rest of the country.

The *Orthodox* churches continue to grow in London even though the number of their churches is shown as decreasing in the last seven years (due to their rationalisation of what "churches" were included in their annual Year Book, as described in Chapter 1). This is partly because of immigration, but also because of their style of spirituality. A significant proportion of total English Orthodox church attendance is focussed within London – about two-thirds of the total in England. However, unlike most denominations, their attendance is much, much smaller than their membership – in 2012 it was only 6% of their members who might attend on an average Sunday. Easter services especially are attended by much larger numbers. It is easy to think of the Orthodox community as small, but in reality it is huge, and larger than the Methodists, for example.

The *Pentecostal* churches are, of course, hugely important to the London scene. Not only do they make up a third of the total attendance, being collectively larger than the Roman

Catholics in the city for the first time in history, but they have grown at a huge rate – 50% in just seven years. Their rate of growth is forecast to slow down quite considerably, however, as a degree of consolidation will probably set in, many, but not all, of these being Black Majority Churches. There are many significant groups with over 100 congregations. While the Redeemed Christian Church of God is the largest (and active academically[34]), other denominations like the Church of God of Prophecy, the Church of Pentecost, the Mountain of Fire churches are also important, as well as the more traditional and long-standing denominations like the New Testament Church of God, Elim and the Assemblies of God. Yet there are literally hundreds and hundreds of individual Black churches, many from a West Indian base and others from an African background, in the capital. Many are small – a sixth (about 250) have 25 or fewer coming on a Sunday – but equally there are about the same number which have more than 200 every week. A few are very large with more than 3,000 people.

The *United Reformed Church* (URC), like the Methodists, has also seen decline in the number attending in the capital over the past 30 years. The number of their churches has reduced, but their average congregation has dropped more – in 1979 they averaged 107 per church, in 2012 about half this number, with 56 people. Like the Methodists they are more represented in other parts of England than in London – 2% to 1%, but the URC's London congregations are bigger than those elsewhere.

Finally, Table 3.3 gives details of the many other *Smaller Denominations* that exist in Britain, and in London. This group is made up of several major denominations, such as the Salvation Army, the Religious Society of Friends, the various Lutheran groups, the Seventh-Day Adventists (at least half of which are effectively BMCs), many Local Ecumenical Partnerships, etc. The most important group within this category, however, in the sense that it has blossomed hugely over the past few years, are the churches for overseas immigrants, details of which were given in Chapter 1. As a consequence of this huge growth, attendance has doubled, but is likely to reduce in the next few years as immigrants move out of London, or to larger churches, or, influenced by secular English culture perhaps, sadly, cease their churchgoing habit altogether. Collectively this group has an especially large proportion of smaller churches – four-fifths are under 100 in size and a quarter 25 or fewer, and this also puts their survival more at risk.

Figure 3.4 graphs the changes to the three largest denominational groups, and all the rest.

Figure 3.4: Church attendance in London by major denominational group, 1979-2020E

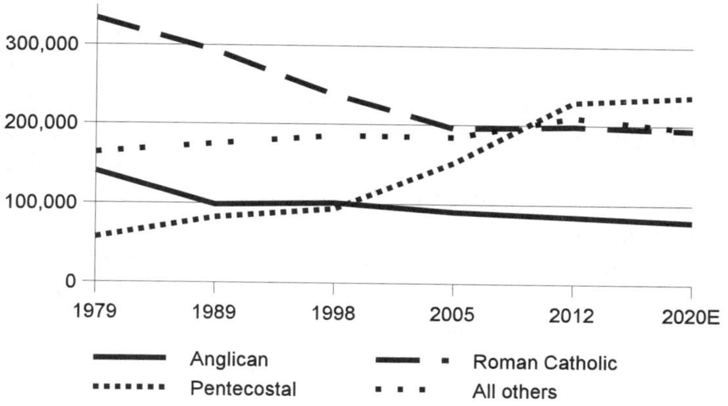

Size of church

The size of churches in Greater London has only been analysed three times in the last 30 years – in 1989, 2005 (partially) and 2012. The data is shown in Tables 3.5 and 3.6:

Table 3.5: Size of churches in Greater London, number and percentages

Year	Under 26	26 to 50	51 to 100	101 to 200	Over 200	Total
1989	130	550	910	1,180	780	3,550
2005	410	740	1,100	980	860	4,090
2012	590	870	1,220	990	1,120	4,790
As percentage of total						
1989	*4*	*15*	*26*	*33*	*22*	*100*
2005	*10*	*18*	*27*	*24*	*21*	*100*
2012	*12*	*18*	*26*	*21*	*23*	*100*

Table 3.5 shows three things about London's churches:

- The number of congregations with 100 or fewer people in them increased between 1989 and 2005, but has remained at almost the same percentage, 56%, in 2012. However, the smallest congregations (25 or under) are increasing fastest.
- The number of congregations with between 100 and 200 people decreased between 1989 and 2005, but has remained about the same between 2005 and 2012.
- The number of larger churches is increasing, though remaining about the same proportion of the whole.

Table 3.6: Size of churches in Greater London greater than 200 people, number and percentages

Year	201 to 300	301 to 400	401 to 500	501 to 800	Over 800	Total
1989	270	100	110	190	110	780
2012	480	160	120	220	140	1,120
As percentage of total						
1989	*8*	*3*	*3*	*5*	*3*	*22*
2012	*10*	*3*	*2*	*5*	*3*	*23*

Table 3.6 shows it is the churches with between 200 and 300 people who have increased the most rapidly, almost doubling in the 23 years shown. The Table does not show that, in 1989, virtually all the 110 very large churches were Roman Catholic, 105 out of the 110, and the other five were Anglican churches. In 2012 only about two-thirds of the 140 very large churches were Roman Catholic (so a smaller number than in 1989), about a third of the rest Anglican, a third Pentecostal and the remaining third a mix of the remaining denominations, including, in

particular, New Churches, Baptist and the Orthodox.

These very large churches may be only 3% of all of London's churches in 2012 but they account for 12% of all attendance: hence their importance. In 1989, half of all the very large churches (800 plus) in England were located in London; and, in 2012, probably a similar proportion were, showing larger churches are increasing elsewhere also.

These figures relate to normal, average, Sunday attendance. Some churches in a certain area, however, deliberately meet together from time to time, naturally making their combined congregation much larger, and giving a feeling of "togetherness". Thus, for example, churches in Southall in the Borough of Ealing met for a "Southall Praise" in October 2012; more than 500 Christians from quite different ethnic backgrounds worshipped together.[35]

The two Tables show the number of churches counted in different years. They do not indicate how far these churches had grown, or declined, or remained static in that period. A study of the churches in the Anglican Diocese of London measured this across the years 2003 to 2010. For the 311 churches for which the researchers had data, they found the total congregations of churches with a congregation of under 50 had grown by 35%; those with individual congregations between 50 and 99 people had seen collective growth of 9%; those whose Sunday attendance was between 100 and 199 people had collectively declined by 1%; those with congregations between 200 and 900 had collectively declined 7%; while those with congregations over 900 (three churches in this case) had collectively grown 7%. This clearly indicates that smaller churches (under 100) tend to be thriving, middle-size churches are struggling, while the largest churches are also growing. How far the overall results are influenced by a few churches in each category, which for some reason have seen outstanding gains or declines in the relevant period, is not known.[36]

Information on one large Anglican church in the north London

Borough of Haringey across several years was kindly provided. The congregation was of the order of 700 people and, while this number had fluctuated somewhat from year to year, over the seven years 2005 to 2012 it had remained largely static (that is, within 10% in the overall period), and its percentage of children under 16 was 19%, virtually the same as the average for that Borough.[37]

Churchmanship

As explained in Chapter 1, the ethos or churchmanship of London churches and churchgoers differs vastly from the rest of England (Table 1:10). Table 3.7 gives the attendance numbers corresponding to the church numbers in that earlier Table.

Table 3.7: Churchmanship of London churchgoers, 1989-2020E

Churchmanship London	Anglo-Catholic	Broad	Catholic	Evangelical Broad	Evangelical Mainstream	Evangelical Charismatic	Evangelical Total	Liberal	Low Church	Others	Total
1989	16,400	24,900	301,500	37,100	67,300	112,400	216,800	46,300	19,600	24,100	649,600
1998	20,000	17,700	194,700	17,900	126,700	121,200	265,800	51,000	30,600	38,100	617,900
2005	20,700	23,900	191,800	16,300	137,700	135,300	289,300	38,400	26,800	32,100	623,000
% change 2005-12	*+10%*	*-2%*	*+2%*	*-5%*	*+24%*	*+41%*	*+30%*	*+3%*	*+5%*	*+7%*	*+16%*
2012	**22,700**	**23,400**	**195,900**	**15,500**	**170,800**	**191,000**	**377,300**	**39,600**	**28,100**	**34,500**	**721,500**
2020E	22,300	21,900	187,800	12,300	175,100	196,000	383,400	35,000	24,500	29,200	704,100
As percentage of Total											
1989	*3*	*4*	*46*	*6*	*10*	*17*	*33*	*7*	*3*	*4*	*100*
1998	*3*	*3*	*32*	*3*	*20*	*20*	*43*	*8*	*5*	*6*	*100*
2005	*3*	*4*	*31*	*3*	*22*	*22*	*47*	*6*	*4*	*5*	*100*
2012	***3***	***3***	***27***	***2***	***24***	***26***	***52***	***6***	***4***	***5***	***100***
2020E	*3*	*3*	*27*	*1*	*25*	*28*	*54*	*5*	*4*	*4*	*100*
Rest of England 2005	*5*	*11*	*26*	*6*	*18*	*14*	*38*	*10*	*7*	*3*	*100*
All England 2005	*5*	*9*	*27*	*6*	*18*	*16*	*40*	*9*	*7*	*3*	*100*

Table 3.7 reflects the huge growth – by almost a third, 30% – in

the number of Evangelicals between 2005 and 2012, as the very large majority of BMCs and many of the immigrant churches are Evangelical, and, if not, tend to be Catholic (hence the growth of the Catholic group also). The Anglo-Catholics have also grown, reflecting a key emphasis of many of the churches in the Diocese of London. The Liberals and Low Church have also grown over these seven years, but are likely to drop back slightly in the years ahead as they are declining quite rapidly nationally.[38]

In 2012 Evangelicals made up just over half (52%) of all the church attenders in London for the first time, a proportion much greater than in England generally where, outside London, they are only 38% of the total. There are few Broad Evangelicals in London, and the Mainstream and Charismatic Evangelicals are almost evenly split. (For clarification on these terms please see footnote 39). Charismatic Evangelicals are markedly much stronger in London than in the rest of England (22% to 14% in 2005).

There are far fewer Broad and Liberal churchgoers in London pro rata than in the rest of England (8% to 21%), partly because many rural churches are often described as Broad. The proportion of Catholics in London, however, corresponds closely to the rest of the country – "Catholic" here meaning a churchmanship, not just the Roman Catholic denomination. A number of Anglican and Methodist churches describe themselves as "Catholic", using the word in its sense of "universal" (as in the Nicene Creed "... one holy, catholic and apostolic church ...").

Anglo-Catholics are usually Anglicans following some aspects of Roman Catholicism and "often ally themselves with Evangelicals to defend traditional teachings on sexual morality," although some would be closer to those following liberal theology.[40]

The 2012 Census shows there are four broadly equal groups of Christians in London – the Catholics, Mainstream Evangelicals, Charismatic Evangelicals and all the rest.

Table 3.8: Total church attendance by London Borough, 1989 to 2012

London Borough	Churchgoers				Change %			% of population			
	1989	1998	2005	**2012**	89-98	98-05	05-12	1989	1998	2005	2012
Camden	15,700	15,600	20,400	**21,700**	*-1*	*31*	***6***	*9.1*	*8.4*	*9.3*	***9.8***
City of London	5,200	4,400	4,100	**5,100**	*-15*	*-7*	***24***	*124.5*	*88.5*	*47.1*	***69.2***
City of Westminster	31,500	25,900	28,500	**33,400**	*-15*	*10*	***17***	*17.9*	*11.8*	*12.3*	***15.2***
Hackney	9,700	11,700	17,800	**16,100**	*21*	*52*	***-10***	*6.3*	*6.1*	*8.5*	***6.5***
Hammersmith & Fulham	11,200	9,500	9,900	**10,500**	*-15*	*4*	***6***	*7.5*	*6.1*	*5.6*	***5.8***
Haringey	17,400	19,400	20,200	**25,900**	*11*	*4*	***28***	*8.5*	*8.8*	*8.9*	***10.2***
Islington	11,200	10,500	13,200	**13,900**	*-6*	*28*	***5***	*6.7*	*5.9*	*7.3*	***6.7***
Kensington & Chelsea	23,500	25,000	27,300	**28,800**	*6*	*9*	***5***	*16.8*	*14.8*	*14.7*	***18.2***
Lambeth	21,600	16,800	19,600	**31,300**	*-22*	*17*	***60***	*8.7*	*6.3*	*7.3*	***10.3***
Lewisham	34,000	28,000	27,200	**31,400**	*-18*	*-3*	***15***	*14.6*	*11.5*	*10.9*	***11.4***
Newham	9,400	10,100	12,100	**16,100**	*7*	*20*	***33***	*4.4*	*4.4*	*4.9*	***5.2***
Southwark	23,700	23,900	26,000	**39,400**	*1*	*9*	***52***	*10.8*	*10.4*	*10.1*	***13.7***
Tower Hamlets	10,700	11,000	11,700	**14,900**	*3*	*6*	***27***	*6.6*	*6.1*	*5.6*	***5.9***
Wandsworth	26,800	27,900	27,700	**32,400**	*4*	*-1*	***17***	*10.5*	*10.6*	*10.0*	***10.6***
Inner London	251,600	239,700	265,700	**320,900**	***-5***	***11***	***21***	***11.1***	***8.9***	***9.0***	***9.9***

Barking & Dagenham	10,200	8,500	7,400	**9,700**	-17	-13	**31**	7.0	5.5	4.5	**5.2**
Barnet	15,300	18,700	19,000	**21,900**	22	2	**15**	5.2	5.7	5.8	**6.1**
Bexley	16,200	12,400	10,000	**11,100**	-23	-19	**11**	7.5	5.7	4.5	**4.8**
Brent	35,000	39,700	39,700	**41,600**	13	0	**5**	14.3	15.8	14.7	**13.4**
Bromley	31,400	24,000	20,000	**23,900**	-24	-17	**20**	10.7	8.1	6.6	**7.7**
Croydon	44,000	34,600	28,700	**35,500**	-21	-17	**24**	13.9	10.3	8.4	**9.8**
Ealing	20,900	19,700	20,100	**23,600**	-6	2	**17**	7.5	6.6	6.6	**7.0**
Enfield	32,300	37,000	37,400	**39,600**	15	1	**6**	12.4	14.0	13.3	**12.7**
Greenwich	17,400	14,500	14,600	**19,100**	-17	1	**31**	8.3	6.8	6.4	**7.5**
Harrow	26,400	27,000	26,100	**26,400**	2	-3	**1**	13.1	12.9	12.2	**11.0**
Havering	19,400	18,500	17,100	**16,300**	-5	-8	**-5**	8.4	8.2	7.5	**6.9**
Hillingdon	19,600	23,200	22,100	**24,600**	18	-5	**11**	8.4	9.3	8.8	**9.0**
Hounslow	10,700	12,500	13,800	**15,900**	17	10	**15**	5.2	5.9	6.5	**6.3**
Kingston upon Thames	15,800	15,600	14,800	**14,800**	-1	-5	**0**	11.8	10.7	9.7	**9.2**
Merton	14,800	11,200	11,300	**14,700**	-24	1	**30**	8.7	6.1	5.8	**7.4**
Redbridge	22,800	18,400	14,400	**15,400**	-19	-22	**4**	10.0	8.0	5.8	**5.2**
Richmond upon Thames	17,500	14,500	13,200	**14,600**	-17	-9	**11**	10.8	7.8	7.2	**7.8**
Sutton	15,300	12,600	12,800	**14,400**	-18	2	**13**	9.0	7.2	7.2	**7.6**
Waltham Forest	13,000	15,600	14,800	**17,500**	20	-5	**18**	6.1	7.1	6.6	**6.8**
Outer London	398,000	378,200	357,300	**400,600**	**-5**	**-6**	12	**8.9**	**8.5**	**7.9**	8.1
Greater London	649,600	617,900	623,000	**721,500**	**-5**	**1**	16	**9.6**	**8.6**	**8.3**	8.8
% Inner of Total	39%	39%	43%	**44%**							

Distribution of Churchgoers across London

There is one further aspect of churchgoers we need to examine in this chapter – where they are concentrated. Total church attendance by Borough is shown in Table 3.8, together with figures from previous studies, how these have changed and their percentage of the population. They are illustrated by maps in Figures 3.9 and 3.10.

This is an interesting Table, showing a number of important findings.

Inner and Outer London

Over the past 14 years (since 1998), the percentage of London's population attending church has been increasing, with Inner London consistently doing so (8.9% in 1998, 9.0% in 2005, 9.9% in 2012), but Outer London only doing so since 2005, and then only just (8.5% in 1998, 7.9% in 2005, 8.1% in 2012). The Inner London increase is sufficient to make the figure for church attendance across the whole of London increase.

Inner London church attendance is virtually 10% of its entire population (9.9%), a significant percentage, much greater than anywhere else in England, and, furthermore, this increase has itself increased by a fifth (21%) in the last seven years, also a rapid rise. Outer London only increased 12% in the same period. Inner London's population is two-fifths (40%) of that of Greater London as a whole; in churchgoing terms, Inner London accounts for 44% of all London's churchgoers (in 1998 it was only 39%).

Key Boroughs in Inner London

The increase in Inner London is especially due to the Boroughs of Lambeth and Southwark, where church attendance has increased over 50% since 2005. These are two of the three Boroughs which have also seen such a high percentage increase in their number of churches. The third Borough, Newham, has also seen its church attendance rise by a third.

The average size of a church in Lambeth in 2005 was 93; in 2012 it was 115. In Southwark the figures are respectively 131 and 144. Of the 14 Boroughs in Inner London, five have seen the number of churchgoers as a percentage of the population increase in both 2005 (from 1998) and 2012 (from 2005) – Camden, the City of Westminster, Haringey, Lambeth and Newham. Five Boroughs account for half the total Inner London attendance – the City of Westminster, Lambeth, Lewisham and Wandsworth (all 10% each) and Southwark (12%).

The City of London's churchgoers were 69% of its population in 2012, but this is a special case. In 1989 they were 125% – more than the population! This is simply because the City boasts a few very large churches which draw many people in from other areas. The number of people living in the City is small, just over 7,000 people, so the churchgoers average a high percentage. These large churches are an example of what might be called "specialist" or "large city centre" churches catering for an especially eclectic congregation. The City of London has 5% of Inner London's churches, but only 1½% of its churchgoers.

There is also another Inner London Borough which is special – Hackney. Hackney is the only Borough in Inner London where attendance has dropped, some 10%. This is almost entirely due to the fact that between 2005 and 2012 the largest church in Britain, which used to meet in a Hackney warehouse, moved. This church, the Kingsway International Christian Centre, whose Senior Pastor is Matthew Ashimolowo, was started with 300 people in 1992 and grew to 10,000 people by 2003. They asked for permission to build a new church, costing £70 million, but were not allowed to do so (rent from businesses occupying the same area would yield greater money for the Council). As the Olympic Park was being built in the nearby Borough of Newham, they offered to build one of the Olympic Stadiums, to be used for free during the Olympics, if they could have it as their church afterwards, but this too was refused. It was also rejected on appeal. So, while the church's congregation was included in Hackney in the 2005 Census, it has now had to disperse its congregation (totalling some 12,000 people, many of whom are Nigerians[41]) into several large buildings, located in different London Boroughs and, thus, the impact of its size has lessened. It has now moved to Chatham, in Kent.

A request to build a huge mosque in Stratford, Newham, by the Tablighi Jamaat, an Islamic missionary group, was turned down by their local council in December 2012. It would have seated 10,000 worshippers,[42] so the Kingsway decision is not an isolated case.

Key Boroughs in Outer London

Three Boroughs have more than 10% of their population in church on a Sunday – Brent and Enfield (both 13%) and Harrow (12%), the latter percentage boosted by chapel attendance at the independent School. The three Boroughs with lowest attendance (all 5%) are Barking & Dagenham, Bexley and Redbridge.

One Outer Borough saw its number of churchgoers decline – Havering, which was also the only Borough to see more churches close than open between 2005 and 2012. Havering has continuously declined since 1989. Kingston upon Thames[43] had the same number attending church in 2012 as in 2005.

However, three Boroughs saw their attendance increase by 30% or more on 2005, including Barking & Dagenham. The other two were Greenwich and Merton, both of which have seen a substantial number of new churches started in the last seven years. Brent and Enfield also saw an increase of 23% and 26%, respectively. One would expect a natural correlation between more churches and a larger number of churchgoers.

Brent and Enfield each account for 10% of the Outer London attendance and one other Borough has more than 30,000 worshippers – Croydon – 9% of the total.

Growth and Numbers compared

Figures 3.9 and 3.10 illustrate the numbers given in Table 3.8. Figure 3.9 gives the numbers of churchgoers by Borough

Figure 3.9: Numbers attending church, 2012

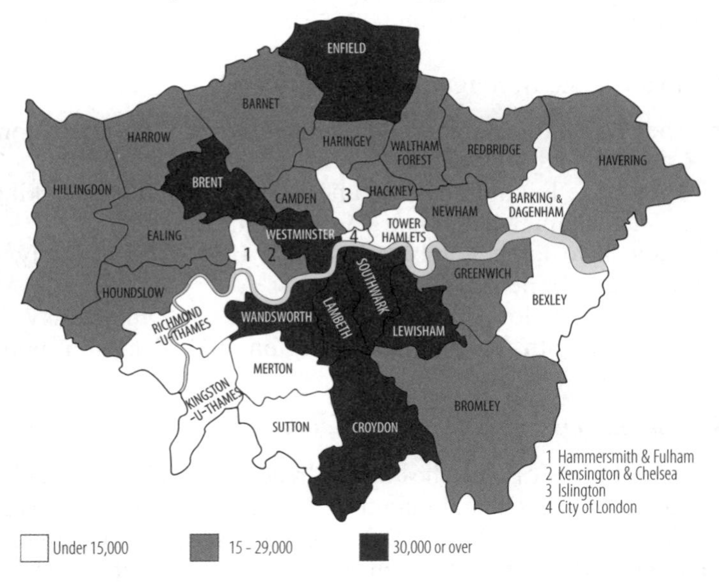

Figure 3.10: Growth in attendance 2005-2012

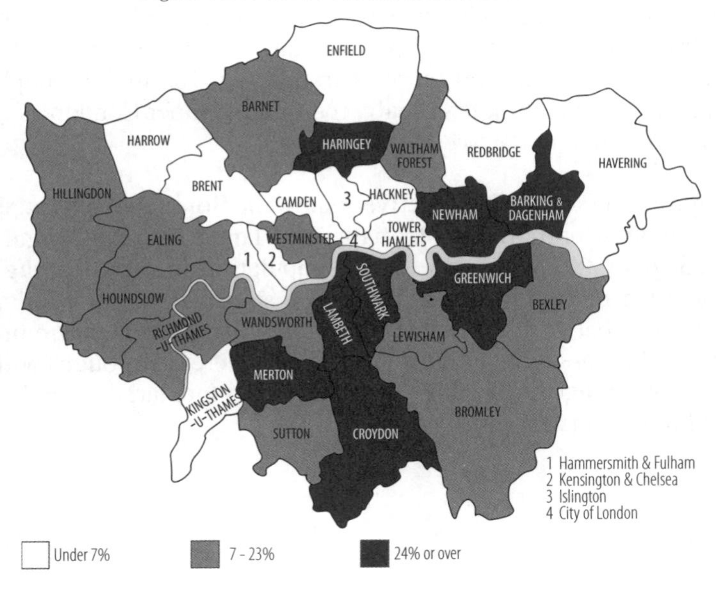

(low, middle and high), and Figure 3.10 shows the growth in attendance between 2005 and 2012 (low, middle and high).

There are some Boroughs where:

- They have large numbers and have grown rapidly – Croydon, Lambeth and Southwark.
- They have low numbers and have grown rapidly – Barking & Dagenham, Merton and Tower Hamlets.
- They have large numbers but have only grown slowly – Brent and Enfield.
- They have low numbers and have grown slowly – Hammersmith & Fulham, Islington and Kingston upon Thames.

Size of church

Details of sizes of churches have already been given in Tables 3.5 and 3.6. The sizes of church by London Borough are given in *Church Statistics* (Page 12.7). There are slightly more smaller churches (100 or under) in Inner London than Outer London (58% to 53%), with an overall average of 55%. There are slightly more larger churches (over 300) in Outer London than in Inner London (15% to 11%), with an overall average of 13%. In between, the proportion of churches with 101 to 300 people in their congregation is virtually the same in Inner London as in Outer London (31% to 32%).

Figures 3.11 and 3.12 respectively show the Boroughs containing the greatest proportions of smaller and larger churches. Figure 3.13 gives the percentage of the population in each Borough attending church in 2012. There is a startlingly clear overlap and logic between these three maps: fewer people means more small churches and very few large ones, whereas Boroughs with many churchgoers are likely to have many more larger churches and fewer smaller ones.

Figure 3:11: Proportions of smaller churches (100 or under), 2012

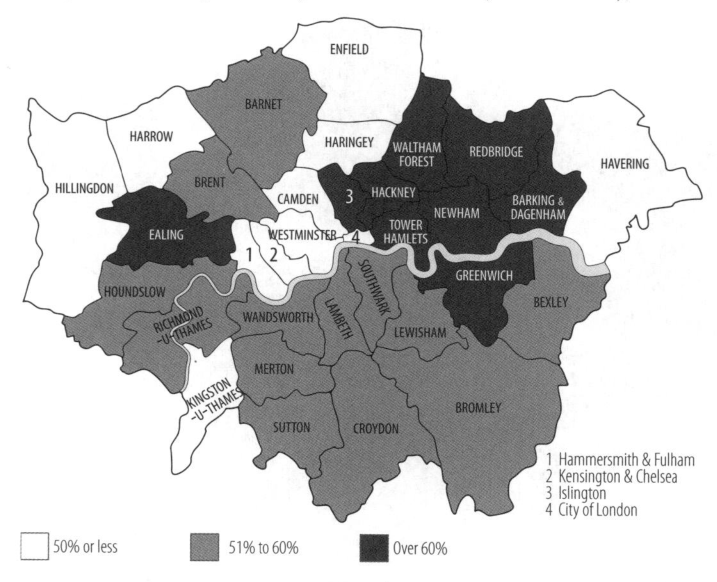

Figure 3.12:Proportions of larger churches (300 or more), 2012

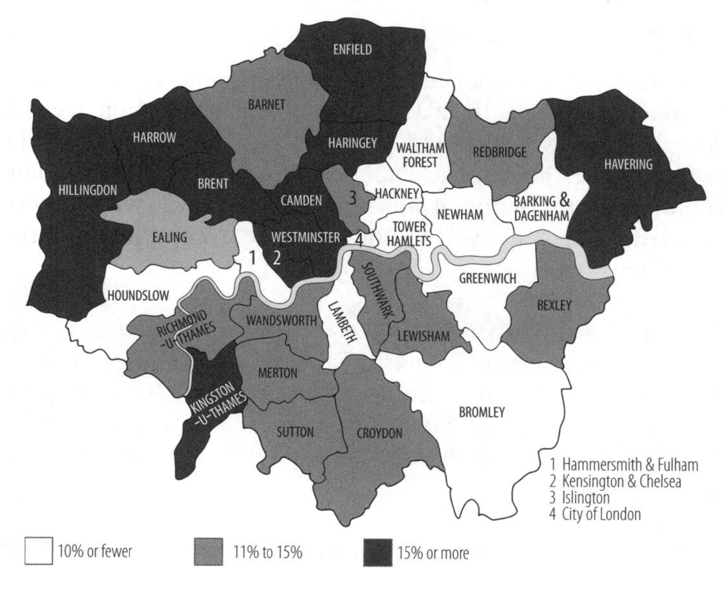

Figure 3.13: Percentage of population attending church, 2012

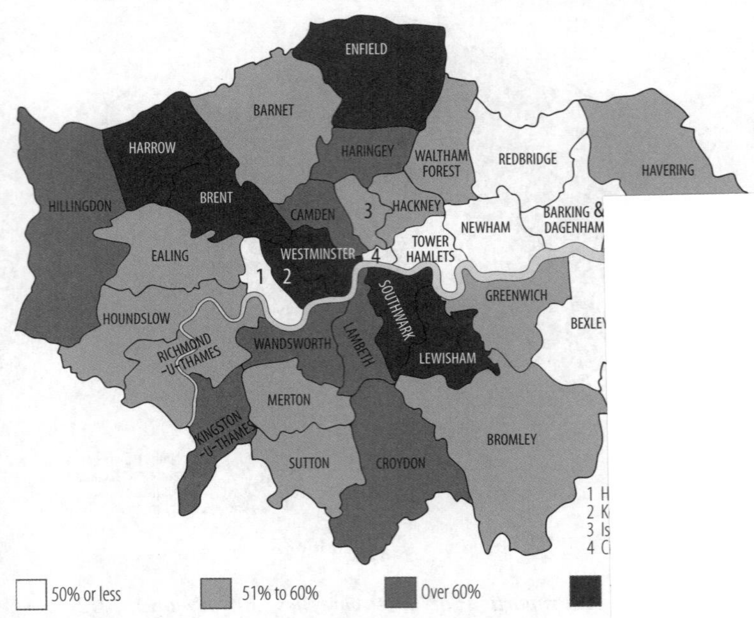

So what does all this say?

This Chapter has looked at the overall church
in Greater London. In 2012, 8.8% of the populat
church on an average Sunday, that is one person
a much higher percentage than pertains in the rest
where, without London, it was only 5.2% in 2012 (
included it is 5.5%). So London is highly exceptio
of religious observance.

Part of that uniqueness comes from the relatively high density of immigrants living in London, many from Christian backgrounds, who are forming new churches (Black Majority Churches, or BMCs). Some, of course, also attend existing churches. The BMCs account for a quarter of all the churches in London.

A second unique feature of London, however, is the relatively high number of very large churches. A fifth, 21%, have congregations over 200 (compared with 12% throughout the whole of England), and of that fifth a third, 7%, have more than 500 people in their congregation. London is host to some of the largest churches in the country. Across its dispersed congregations, the Kingsway International Christian Centre has 12,000 (many of whom are Nigerian), Hillsong in the Dominion Theatre in West London, 6,000, while Anglican churches like Holy Trinity Brompton see 4,000 every week. Some of the BMCs are sizeable also – Kensington Temple (Elim), Ruach Ministries in Brixton, Jesus House for all Nations in Brent and House of Praise in Woolwich have 3,000 to 4,000 each, and there are other, if slightly smaller, Anglican churches such as All Souls, Langham Place and St Helens, Bishopsgate. The Roman Catholics have many churches with total Sunday Mass attendance well into four figures too. These large churches account for half of all London churchgoers.

Yet not all of London churches are growing and doing well. Half of the churches in London are neither larger churches nor BMCs, but just "ordinary" denominational churches frequently well over a century old. Altogether they account for a quarter of the capital's congregations, but this group contains many small churches, some struggling to keep going. One church in eight in London, 12%, has a Sunday congregation of 25 or fewer people, although this is less than half the percentage (28%) across England as a whole.

In denominational terms, the key growth group is the Pentecostals, who comprise a third (32%) of all London's churchgoers, and, in fact, are two-thirds of all the Pentecostals in the country. Their proportion is likely to continue increasing, if more slowly than in the past 15 years. The next largest group is the Roman Catholics, a quarter (27%) of London's church attenders in 2012; they slightly increased over 2005 because of the new immigrants but are generally a decreasing proportion of the whole. After the Roman Catholics come the Anglicans, with a 6% decline in their numbers since 2005, but still 12% of the total. These three denominations, thus, account for 71%

of the total churchgoing in London, with the many remaining denominations collectively forming the other 29%.

The further exceptional feature of London's churchgoing is the fact that over half, 52%, are Evangelical (against 38% in the rest of England): because the large majority of the BMCs are evangelical, and many of the non-Roman Catholic larger churches are also of a similar ethos. While a Catholic churchmanship is not to be totally equated with the Roman Catholic denomination, Catholics are also 27% of the total, meaning that churches of other persuasions combined account for just 21% of the total, whereas, in the country as a whole, 33%. The next largest group in the capital would be the Liberal/Broad group, 9% of the total.

The spread of churchgoers is not uniform across the city. Seven Boroughs (Brent, Enfield, Harrow, Kensington & Chelsea, Lewisham, Southwark, and Westminster) have more than 10% of their population attending church, while others, especially where many are Muslim, have less than 6%. Many of these Boroughs also have a high proportion of larger churches, showing that church size is related to market potential, as might be expected and is highly relevant to church planting strategy. Lambeth and Southwark have an especially high number of BMCs, and these Boroughs and churches in Muslim-dominated Boroughs have seen a fascinating growth in attendance since 2005, demonstrating growth is not invariably related to size of market (also important for church planting strategy).

4

Age and Gender of London's Churchgoers

Nearly three-quarters of a million people may attend church on an average Sunday in London, but how old are they, and are they male or female? This chapter looks at these factors and compares them with previous analyses to demonstrate the trends. As with other aspects of London's church life, the figures about to be given are not necessarily typical of the rest of England. Predictably, the capital is different.

The questionnaire asked for total numbers attending across all services on Sunday, 14 October 2012, or a Sunday near to that one. Some churches took great trouble and counted each service separately, while others estimated the ages and gender of attenders. The form asked whether the figures were estimated or counted, and a statistical test was undertaken to see if the estimated figures were significantly different from the actual. They were not; as in previous Censuses, there was no statistical difference[44] and the estimated figures could, therefore, be added to the counted figures.

Gender

Just over two-fifths of London's churchgoers, 44%, are male, and just under three-fifths, 56%, are female. One or two Methodist churches returned forms indicating some of their attenders had responded they were transsexual or not strictly either male or female, but the numbers are so small as to make no difference in the broad overview.

This 44% is lower than in 2005, when the percentage of males was 48%, but higher than in 1989 when it was 42%. (Gender was not measured in the 1998 study.)

Age groups of churchgoers

The age groups in 2012 were taken as the same groups used in the 2005 English Church Census (to allow comparisons). Figure 4.1 shows the percentages in each group for each Census, with breakdowns for those under 15, and 65 and over, estimated for years before 2005. The actual percentages are given in Table A2 in the Appendix, together with an estimate for 2020.

Figure 4.1: Proportions of Greater London churchgoers by age-group, 1979 to 2012

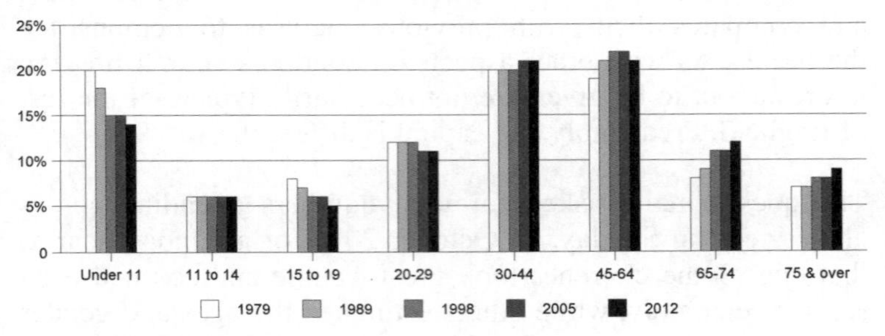

Figure 4.1 shows:

- The proportions of those aged under 11 and aged 15 to 19 have declined for the past 33 years and are likely to continue to do so.
- The proportions of those aged 11 to 14 remained at 6% throughout the period 1979 to 2012, and the proportions of those in their 20s also changed little. Likewise, the proportion of those aged 30 to 44 did not change much.
- The proportions of those aged 45 to 64, 65 to 74 and 75 and over all increased steadily since 1979, though the percentage aged 45-64 dropped 1% in 2012. Since these are all the older age-groups, it means the percentage of churchgoers 45 or over increased from 34% in 1979 to 42% in 2012.

With fewer younger people attending, and more older people, the average age of attenders is increasing. In 1979 the average

age was 35; in 2012 it was 41.

Table 4.2 shows how the 2012 percentages compare with the population:

Table 4.2: London churchgoers as percentage of London's population

Age	Under 11 %	11-14 %	15-19 %	20-29 %	30-44 %	45-64 %	65-74 %	75-84 %	85 & over %	Base =100%
London population	14	4	6	18	25	21	6	4	2	8.2 m
London Churchgoers	14	6	5	11	21	22	12	7	2	0.7 m
London churchgoers as % of population	**9**	**13**	**7**	**6**	**7**	**9**	**19**	**16**	**12**	**9**
Rest of England pop.	13	5	6	13	20	26	9	6	2	44.8 m
English population	13	5	6	14	21	25	9	5	2	53.0 m

Table 4.2 shows that an exceptionally high proportion of 11 to 14 year olds attend church in London, due in part to church attendance at independent schools, and perhaps to the need for choristers in the capital's Cathedrals. While the lowest proportion is of those in their 20s, this is in fact double the percentage across England in 2005. Almost one in five, 19%, of those in their "Third Age" (65 to 74) in London go to church, double the city's average and three times the national average.

Inner and Outer London

As might be expected, the percentages by age group were not the same for Inner and Outer London, indicated in Table 4.3:

Table 4.3: Proportions of churchgoers by age group in Inner and Outer London, 2012

Age group	<11 %	11-14 %	15-19 %	20-29 %	30-44 %	45-64 %	65-74 %	75-84 %	85 & over %	Average age	Base =100%
Inner	13	6	5	14	21	21	11	7	2	40	320,900
Outer	15	7	5	9	21	21	13	7	2	41	400,600
Total	14	6	5	11	21	22	12	7	2	41	721,500

Table 4.3 shows that while Outer London has a greater number of children in church than Inner London and more people in their "Third Age" (65 to 74), the absolutely key difference is the

proportion of those aged 20 to 29 who are much more likely to go to church in Inner London. More than half of those in their 20s going to church in Greater London go to an Inner London church, perhaps like Hillsong or Holy Trinity Brompton [HTB], both of which have an unusually high number of young people. Inner London has a slightly greater proportion of boys under 15 in church than girls (21% to 18%); might this be because of the Anglican Cathedrals and other choirs operating in Inner London (though many such choirs do have girls as well)?[45] "Surveys by the National Health Service show that Londoners aged between 11 and 15 are less likely to smoke than are youngsters in every other English region. They drink alcohol much more rarely"[46] also. Might that be because so many go to church? Ealing has lowest rate of substance abuse in London – is that because it is heavily Asian?

Male and Female percentages

The proportion of churchgoers in Greater London by gender and age group is shown in Table 4.4. The percentage of men in the church aged 65 or over is less than the proportion of women for reasons of ordinary mortality: therefore, the average age of the female attender is greater than the male (42 to 39).

For those under 20, the percentage of males in the church is greater than the percentage of females, 29% young men to 24% young women. This was true for 11 to 19 year olds in 2005 also, and true for 15 to 19 year olds across English churchgoers as a whole.

So why is this? There is no relevant known research, but one suggestion is that, as far as the older girls are concerned, they are more sexually active than boys (and more lose their virginity earlier[47]), and churches generally look on such behaviour disapprovingly, so teenage females are more likely to leave. In a 2005 survey of 1,300 teenagers, half of whom identified as being committed Christians, 38% of females and 18% of males said they had had sexual intercourse by the age of 16, and 43% of females and 33% of males by the age of 17. Of those who had become Christians at 12 or later, 37% had had intercourse, but only 12% of those who had become Christian before 12.[48]

Table 4.4: Proportions of churchgoers by age group by gender in Greater London, 2012

Age group	<11 %	11-14 %	15-19 %	20-29 %	30-44 %	45-64 %	65-74 %	75-84 %	85 & over %	Average age	Base =100%
Male	16	7	6	11	20	21	11	6	2	39	316,000
Female	13	6	5	11	21	22	13	7	2	42	405,500
Total	14	6	5	11	21	22	12	7	2	41	721,500

There are more women churchgoers aged 30 to 64 in Outer London than in Inner London (43% to 41%), and more women aged 65 and over (22% to 19%), suggesting perhaps more families, or at least couples, going to church in Outer London. The 2011 Population Census showed more one person households in Inner London than Outer London; presumably, many of these are single women.

Comparison with rest of England

The ages of people going to church in London contrast sharply to the rest of England as can be seen in Table 4.5. In 2005, the latest year for which figures for the rest of the country are available, 27% of London's churchgoers were under 20; comparing with 25% in the rest of England, showing there were slightly more children going to church in the capital pro rata than elsewhere, but as the 2012 percentage for under 20s has dropped to 25%, this difference may be less than before (the comparator percentage for 2012 not being known).

Table 4.5: Percentage of churchgoers in London and elsewhere in England, 2005

Age group	<11 %	11-14 %	15-19 %	20-29 %	30-44 %	45-64 %	65-74 %	75-84 %	85 & over %	Aver age	Base (=100%)
London 2005	15	6	6	11	21	22	11	6	2	41	623,000
Rest of England	13	7	5	6	14	24	18	10	3	46	2,543,200
All England	13	6	5	7	16	24	17	10	2	45	3,166,200

However, the percentage of churchgoers in their 20s in London, 11% in 2005 (and 12% in 2012) is one of the key differences – double the percentage of churchgoers elsewhere. Likewise the percentage of people aged 30 to 44 years of age (the age of many parents) at 21% of London's churchgoers in 2005 (and the same in 2012) compares with just 14% across the rest of the country. So proportionately fewer families are going to church outside London.

The other key difference is in the proportion of older people. A fifth (19%) of churchgoers in London in 2005 were 65 or over (21% in 2012). This compares with a massive 31% outside the capital. No wonder the average age of a churchgoer outside London in 2005 was 46, compared with 41 in London (and still 41 in 2012).

That so many more people aged 30 to 44 are going to church in the city might imply more London couples are childless than couples elsewhere, but this is not true. The 2011 Population Census shows 35% of families (including cohabiting couples) have no children; in Greater London the percentage is virtually the same at 34%. So, the proportion of children in church being much the same as elsewhere, despite the proportion of families being so much higher can only mean London's families are less good at bringing their children to church: an intriguing fact – or that they have smaller families. This is an area where further research would be helpful.

So London has more families in church than in the rest of England pro rata to the number of churchgoers, more people in their 20s, the same proportion of children, and far fewer elderly people. A third (32% in 2005 and in 2012) of London's churchgoers are aged 20 to 44, compared to a fifth in the rest of England (20% in 2005).

This age group straddles what are sometimes called the Gen X and Gen Y age groups. Gen Xers were born between 1965 and 1983, making them between 29 and 47 in 2012; Gen Yers were born between 1984 and 2002, making them between 10 and

28 in 2012. So, the higher numbers of London's churchgoers are the younger Gen Xers and the older Gen Yers. Part of the general characteristics of these age groups, which may or may not be true of churchgoers, are:

- Many single-parent families; much co-habitation; much divorce; recreational sex.
- Peer values crucial; designer label fans; brand-conscious.
- Brought up with sophisticated computers and the web, Facebook, Twitter, etc.
- Tolerant towards drug-taking, homosexuality and film violence.
- Many have only a vague spiritual compass, and will think of themselves as "spiritual" rather than "religious".
- Independent; like working in financial businesses or for themselves.
- High risk-takers; high levels of stress; only willing to make short-term commitments; focussed on self-fulfilment.
- Happy to work as, and with, a team.
- Apolitical, and sceptical of government; respectful of professionals; see older people as past their sell-by date![49]

The various percentages in Tables 4.3, 4.4 and 4.5 are illustrated in Figure 4.6.

Figure 4.6: Age of churchgoers in Greater London and England

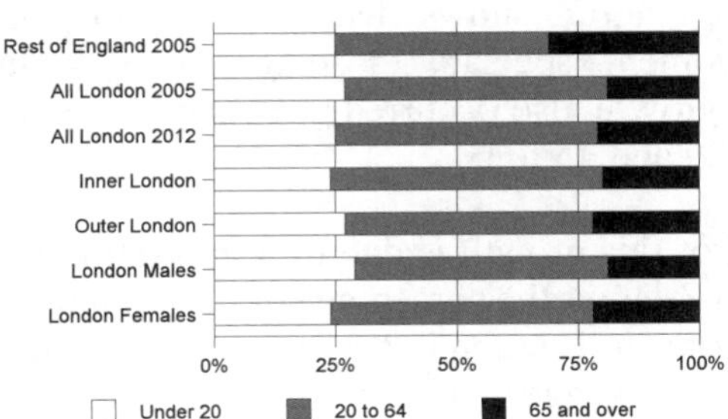

Gains and losses

One further useful calculation is to look, in detail, by age and gender, at where the gains and losses were made between 2005 and 2012. We know the total attendance in 2005 was 623,000 people and in 2012 was 712,500, an overall gain of 98,500 people, or an average of 14,100 per year. Of those gains, a fifth (18%) were men and four-fifths (82%) were women.

These gains were fairly uniform across all age groups with one exception – the number of teenagers who joined the church was only about a fifth of those in the other age groups in total. The detailed calculation is shown in Table A5 in the Appendix, and is graphed in Figure 4.7.

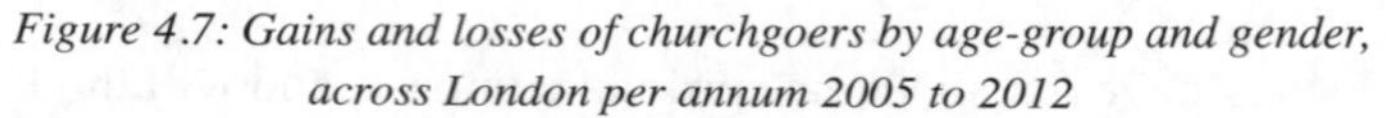

Figure 4.7: Gains and losses of churchgoers by age-group and gender, across London per annum 2005 to 2012

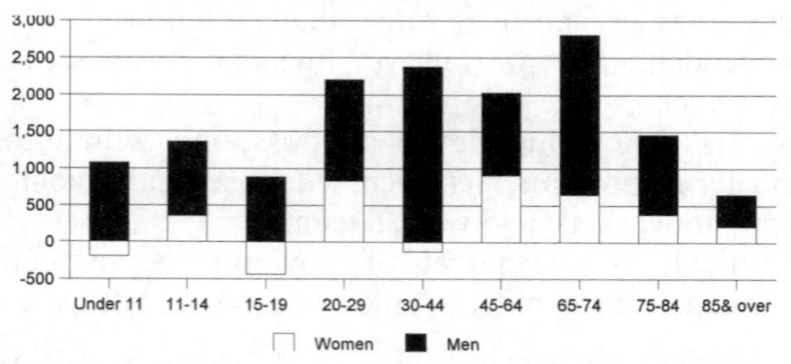

Figure 4.7 shows that the growth in attendance between 2005 and 2012 is spread across all age groups, though not both genders. Males aged under 11, 15 to 19 and 30 to 44 all fell slightly. The diagram shows clearly the majority of the growth is among women, especially those aged 30 to 44 and 65 to 74. Significant growth also occurred, across both genders, of those aged 20 to 29 and 45 to 64.

How much of this growth is due to immigration is not known, but Figure 4.8 shows the percentage of immigrants by age group who have come to London in the last decade.[50] Correlating this with Figure 4.7 suggests that some of the growth in children under 11 and some of the growth among those in their 20s could be due to the influx of immigrants, but their impact on other age-groups would be much less.

Figure 4.8: Age of immigrants in London, 2011

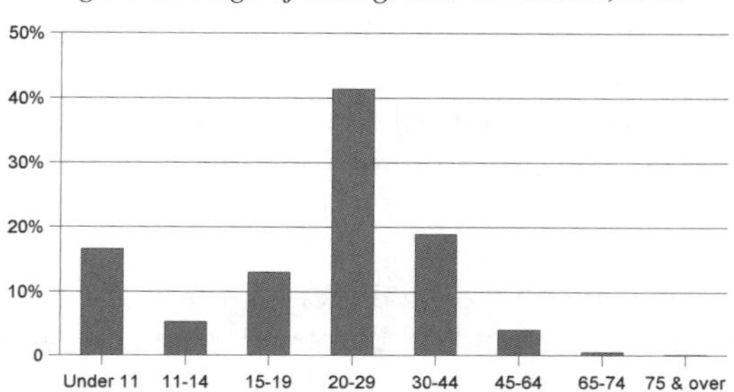

Focus on youth

It is always important to examine the behaviour of the next generation. The proportions under 20 in 2012 are less than in previous years (while the proportion of older people has increased) as Figure 4.1 shows. Nevertheless, the percentage of attenders under 20 is slightly greater in London than in the rest of England (27% to 25%), from Table 4.5. Table 4.3 shows that the proportion under 20 in Inner London is smaller than in Outer London (24% to 27%), but this was true also in 2005, and is a consequence of there being so many people in their 20s attending in Inner London (which pushes other percentages down slightly).

Of greater concern is the disparity with gender, with 29% of males attending church in Greater London in 2012 being under 20 against 24% of females, although in terms of actual numbers, there are more women in this age group in church now than in 2005 and fewer men (Figure 4.6 and Table A5). However, while this age group accounts for 27% of all attenders, it only accounted for 19% of the increase between 2005 and 2012. (Those 65 and over are only 21% of all attenders but accounted for 35% of the increase between 2005 and 2012).

What this all means is that while child attendance in London may be regarded as fairly healthy, and better than elsewhere, numbers are not growing as fast as with older people pro rata, and that is especially true with women under 20: an obvious cause for concern.

The proportions of churches with NO children or youth are lower than in England generally in 2005. Overall, a quarter (25%) of churches had no-one at all attending under the age of 20, this percentage being only half of that (46%) across England as a whole in 2005. The 2012 figure for Greater London churches was:

- 17% had no-one attending under 11 years of age
- 33% had no-one attending between 11 and 14, and
- 39% had no-one attending between 15 and 19.

The respective 2005 percentages across England were 39%, 49% and 59%, reflecting the lack of young people in thousands of rural churches. Yet a sixth (17%) of churches with no children, a third (33%) with no tweenagers, and two-fifths (39%) with no teenagers in the capital is clearly not good news. The percentages are slightly better for Inner London and for young women.[51]

Churches will invariably have special activities for their children (under 10), whether this be called "Sunday School" or a more imaginative name. The very large majority of churches, 97%, also had their children in their main church service for at least part of the time.

Age by size of church

In general terms, the smaller the church, the older the people who worship there. The smallest churches, those with 25 or fewer on a Sunday, have a third (34%) of their congregation aged 65 or over. This may not be unusual for rural churches, but it is relatively unusual in London. One church in eight, 12%, is this small, collectively accounting for just 2% of the total congregation. This 34% is almost twice the percentage of that age in larger churches (19%); these details coming from the figures in Table 4.9, and which is illustrated in Figure 4.10.

Table 4.9: Proportion of congregation in each age-group by size of London church, 2012

Size of church	<11 %	11-14 %	15-19 %	20-29 %	30-44 %	45-64 %	65-74 %	75-84 %	85 & over %	Average age	Base =100%
25 or under	*10*	*4*	*3*	*7*	*14*	*28*	*19*	*11*	*4*	*50*	10,600
26 to 50	*14*	*6*	*4*	*8*	*16*	*25*	*15*	*9*	*3*	*44*	43,300
51 to 100	*16*	*7*	*4*	*9*	*18*	*24*	*13*	*7*	*2*	*41*	101,500
101 to 200	*16*	*7*	*5*	*10*	*20*	*21*	*12*	*7*	*2*	*40*	146,200
Over 200	*13*	*6*	*6*	*12*	*23*	*21*	*11*	*6*	*2*	*40*	419,900
Total	***14***	***6***	***5***	***11***	***21***	***22***	***12***	***7***	***2***	***41***	**721,500**

Table 4.9 shows that the larger the church the greater the proportion of the congregation likely to be teenagers, in their 20s and aged 30 to 44; and the larger the church, the smaller the proportion of those aged 45 or older. The proportion of tweenagers, aged 11 to 14, is about the same whatever the church's size, while churches with attendance between 50 and 200 seem to attract an above average proportion of children under 11.

Two-thirds (65%) of all those in their 20s going to church in London go to larger churches.

Figure 4.10: Proportion of congregation by age-group and by size of church, 2012

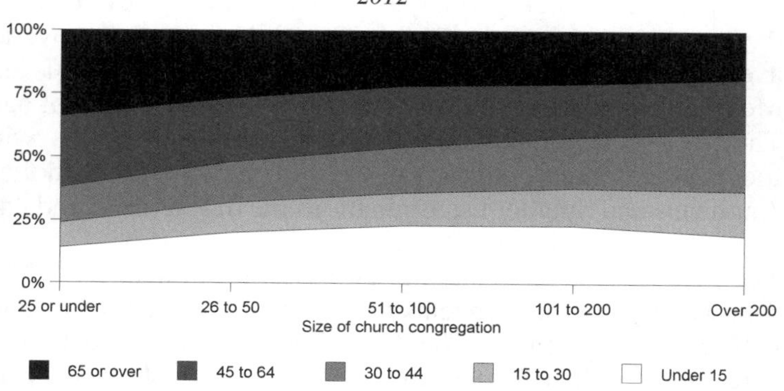

Age of congregations by denomination

Some denominations have much younger congregations than others. The proportions in each age group are shown in Table 4.11 for each denomination, and these are shown also in the chart, Figure 4.12. The actual numbers are given in Table A6 in the Appendix.

Table 4.11: Age of congregation by denomination in percentages, Greater London, 2012

Age-group	Angl'n %	Baptist %	R Cath %	Indep't %	Method. %	New Ch %	Ortho. %	Pente %	URC %	Smaller %	**Total %**
Under 11	*12*	*16*	*13*	*16*	*8*	*16*	*9*	*17*	*13*	*11*	***14***
11-14	*5*	*5*	*5*	*8*	*3*	*5*	*6*	*9*	*4*	*8*	***6***
15-19	*3*	*4*	*4*	*5*	*2*	*4*	*8*	*6*	*1*	*3*	***5***
20-29	*12*	*9*	*9*	*10*	*4*	*20*	*11*	*13*	*5*	*11*	***11***
30-44	*18*	*20*	*18*	*18*	*8*	*25*	*19*	*27*	*10*	*18*	***21***
45-64	*23*	*24*	*21*	*22*	*26*	*19*	*24*	*20*	*21*	*24*	***22***
65-74	*16*	*13*	*17*	*13*	*25*	*7*	*12*	*6*	*21*	*14*	***12***
75-84	*9*	*7*	*10*	*6*	*19*	*3*	*11*	*2*	*18*	*8*	***7***
85 & over	*2*	*2*	*3*	*2*	*5*	*1*	*0*	*0*	*7*	*3*	***2***
Base =100%	84,800	41,900	198,300	29,500	18,300	43,200	19,900	229,000	8,000	48,600	**721,500**
Average age	44	41	45	40	57	35	43	33	53	44	**41**

The youngest congregations are Pentecostal or New Church; the average age is respectively, 33 and 35, against an overall average of 41. The oldest congregations are the URC and Methodists; the respective averages are 53 and 57 years of age. The other six denominations all have an average in the 40s, with Independents the youngest (at 40) and the Roman Catholics, Anglicans and Smaller Denominations the oldest (at 45 and 44).

The Pentecostals have the highest percentage under 20 (32%), followed by the Independents (29%), with the Methodists only half this figure (14%). The New Churches have the highest percentage of their number in their 20s (20%), followed by the Pentecostals (13%) and the Anglicans (12%).

Figure 4.12: Proportion of congregation by age-group and by denomination, 2012

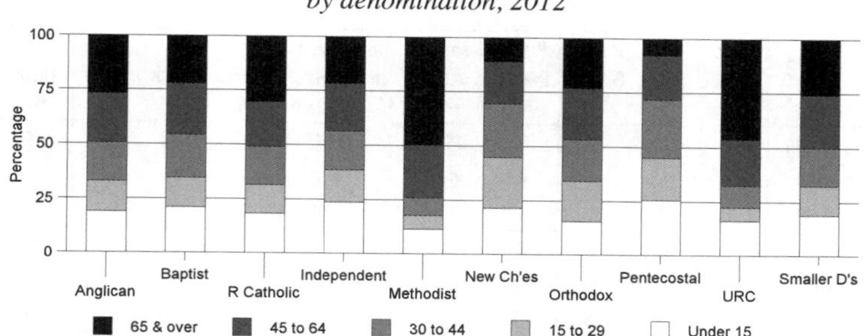

Virtually every denomination has just under a quarter of its congregations aged between 45 and 64. The Roman Catholics have almost a third 65 or over (30%), the next largest being the Anglicans (27%) after the huge percentages of 49% for the Methodists and 46% for the URC.

Age of congregations by churchmanship

Likewise, churchmanship varies by age. Details are given in Table 4.14 and illustrated in Figure 4.13, with the actual figures given in Table A7.

Figure 4.13: Proportion of congregation by age-group and by churchmanship, 2012

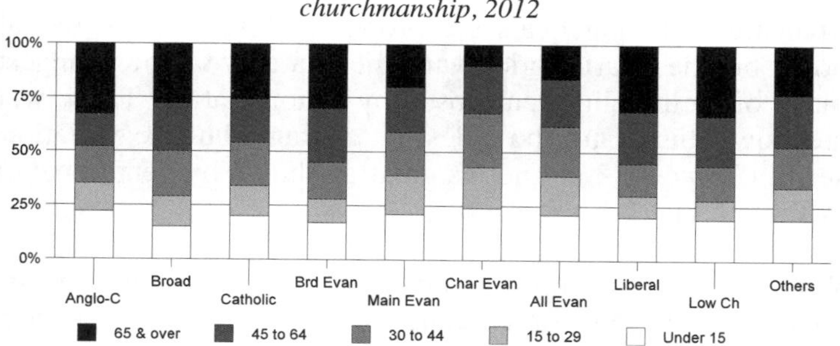

Table 4.14: Proportion of congregation by age-group and by churchmanship, 2012

Age-group	Anglo-Catholic %	Broad %	Roman Catholic %	Broad Evang. %	Mainst. Evan. %	Charis. Evan. %	Total Evan. %	Liberal %	Low Church %	All others %	**Total %**
Under 11	*12*	*10*	*14*	*13*	*15*	*16*	*15*	*15*	*13*	*12*	***14***
11-14	*10*	*5*	*6*	*4*	*6*	*8*	*6*	*5*	*6*	*7*	***6***
15-19	*5*	*3*	*5*	*4*	*4*	*6*	*5*	*3*	*2*	*5*	***5***
20-29	*8*	*11*	*9*	*7*	*14*	*13*	*13*	*7*	*7*	*10*	***11***
30-44	*17*	*21*	*20*	*17*	*20*	*25*	*23*	*15*	*16*	*19*	***21***
45-64	*15*	*22*	*20*	*25*	*21*	*22*	*22*	*24*	*23*	*24*	***22***
65-74	*20*	*16*	*15*	*16*	*12*	*6*	*9*	*17*	*18*	*12*	***12***
75-84	*10*	*9*	*8*	*10*	*6*	*3*	*5*	*11*	*12*	*9*	***7***
85 & over	*3*	*3*	*3*	*4*	*2*	*1*	*2*	*3*	*3*	*2*	***2***
Base =100%	22,700	23,400	195,900	15,500	170,800	191,000	377,300	39,600	28,100	34,500	**721,500**
Average Age	44	45	43	47	40	35	38	46	47	42	**41**

The Anglo-Catholics are the strongest with those aged 11 to 14, perhaps because of their church choirs, but have (with the Low Church) the highest proportion who are 65 or over – a third of their number, 33%. Likewise those who are Broad, Broad Evangelical and Liberal have a high proportion of older people – all 28% or more, against an overall average of 21%. The difference is extremely significant in statistical terms.

Mainstream Evangelicals are probably closest to the overall norm, but the Charismatic Evangelicals are by far the youngest, many of them being Pentecostal by denomination. Those who are Low Church are the oldest on average, but the variations seen in Table 4.13 are not as great as shown by denomination in Table 4.11.

While churchmanship is unquestionably important, in the context of the age of churchgoers, probably the respective denominations give a more coherent story.

Age of congregations by Borough

The proportions by age group for each London Borough are given in a Table in *Church Statistics*. It shows:

- There are far fewer children under 11 attending church in the City of London and the City of Westminster than in other Boroughs (4% and 9% respectively against an overall average for London of 14%), while the Boroughs of Barnet, Hounslow (18% each) and Croydon (19%) have the highest percentages. The 2011 Population Census shows far fewer families with children live in the City (7% to 19%).

- Tweenagers (those aged 11 to 14) are least represented in the City of London (4%) and City of Westminster (2%) and most represented in Harrow (13%), school chapel attendance being compulsory at independent schools such as Harrow. The Boroughs of Ealing, Hackney and Islington all have 9% of their attendance in this age group (against 6% overall).

- Teenage attendance does not vary greatly, from a Tower Hamlets low of 3% to a City of Westminster (8%) and Harrow (12%) high, against 5% overall.

- The parental age group of 30 to 44 varies more in Outer London than Inner London, with a low of 13% in Bexley and Redbridge against a high of 28% each in Greenwich and Hillingdon, with an overall average of 21%.

- The age group of 45 to 64 varies more within Inner London than Outer London. Six Boroughs in Inner London are under 20% but only one in Outer (Brent). Two Boroughs in each have 25% – Haringey and Kensington & Chelsea in Inner London and Barking & Dagenham and Redbridge in Outer London.

- The highest average ages of churchgoers are found in Redbridge (age 48), Kensington & Chelsea (age 46) and Bexley (age 45), while Islington, Harrow and Waltham Forest (at age 35 each) have the lowest.

The percentage of churchgoers in their 20s varies most of all and is illustrated in Figure 4.15 on the next page. The Boroughs with the lowest percentages are Redbridge (5%), Harrow and Hillingdon (each 6%), while the highest is the City of London with 29%, followed by Camden (21%) and the City of

Westminster (20%), against an overall average of 11%. Each of these sizeable percentages are because of large churches in those Boroughs (respectively, St Helen's Bishopsgate, Hillsong, and Holy Trinity Brompton and All Souls, Langham Place). The City of London, City of Westminster, Croydon, Kingston upon Thames and Tower Hamlets have all seen a significant increase in the percentage of their churchgoers who are in their 20s (each at least 4%).

The proportions of churchgoers 65 and over also varies widely, as illustrated in Figure 4.16. A third (34%) of Redbridge's churchgoers are 65 or over, followed by 30% in Kensington & Chelsea and 29% in each of Bexley and Bromley. On the other hand, only 10% of Islington's churchgoers are in this age group, 11% in Waltham Forest, and 12% each in Greenwich and Hounslow.

There are a few Boroughs to support the thesis the church is growing where a greater number of younger attenders is present, and, equally, there are some which do not. Intriguingly, growth appears to be more a matter of denomination, churchmanship or size than location.

Figure 4.15: Percentage of churchgoers aged 20 to 29

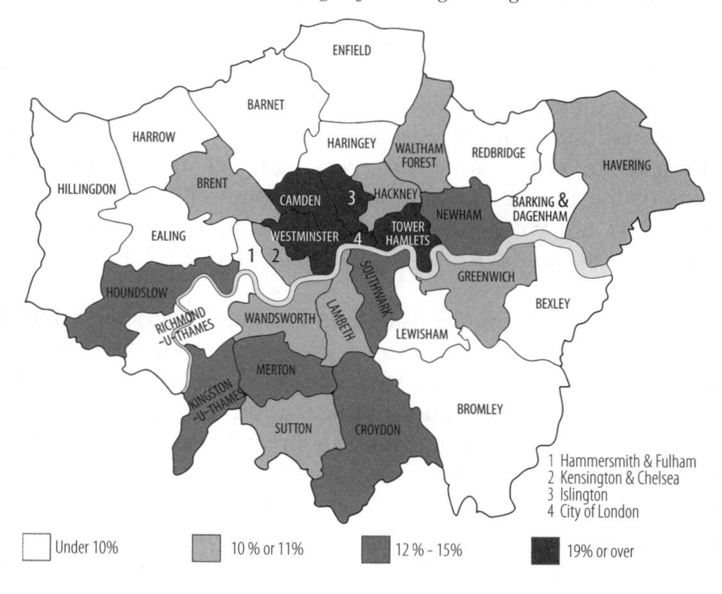

Figure 4.16: Percentage of churchgoers aged 65 and over

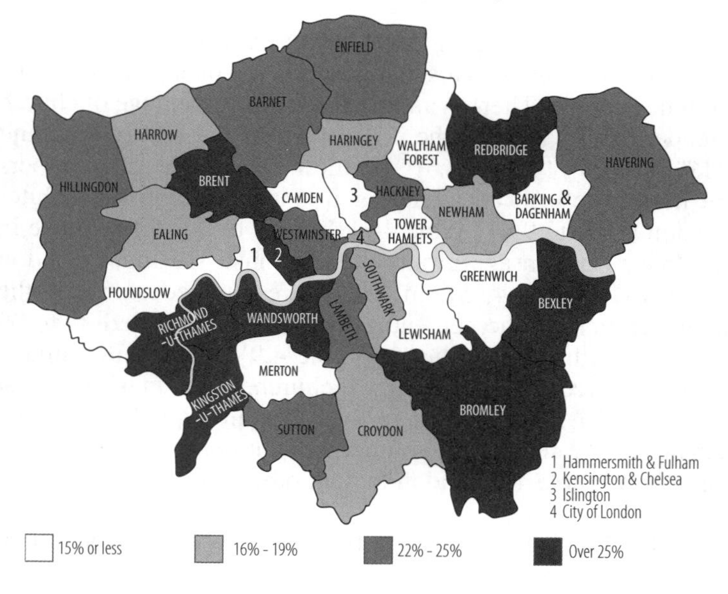

So what does all this say?

A lengthy chapter has been needed to look at the fascinating topic of gender and age of London's churchgoers in 2012. In terms of gender, the male to female ratio is 44:56, similar to the national ratio, but indicating rather more women attending church in the city than seven years ago: because almost five-sixths of the increase in numbers attending church in London since 2005 are women rather than men, and especially those aged 30 to 44 and 65 to 74 [Figure 4.6 and Table A5].

In age terms, the proportions of London's churchgoers under 11 and in their teenage years (15 to 19) has continued to decline, and the proportion who are 65 to 74 and 75 and over has grown [Figure 4.1]. There are more children and more older people in church in Outer London than in Inner London [Table 4.3], but the gender balance is most interesting. A greater proportion of male churchgoers are under 20 than female (29% to 24%) [Table 4.4], the specific reasons for which are unknown, while there is a greater proportion of older women than men, but this is because of normal mortality reasons.

It is the 20 to 29 age group, however, which is especially important in London. This age group helps makes the capital's churches unique. There is almost twice the percentage of church attenders in London in their 20s, than in the rest of England (11% to 6%) [Table 4.5]. Furthermore, those churchgoers are more likely to be attending in Inner London than Outer London (14% to 9%) [Table 4.3]. In fact, two-fifths of those in this Inner London age group attend in just five Inner London Boroughs [Figure 4.15], in which are situated some of the largest churches. The percentage of churchgoers aged 20 to 29 increases with size of church [Table 4.9], there being almost twice the percentage in the largest churches than in the smallest (12% to 7%). Churchgoers in their 20s are equally male and female, unlike the other age groups mentioned in the previous paragraph [Table 4.4], and in fact all other age groups.

The other key factor emerging from the analysis of age is that attenders in some denominations are much older than others. Half (49%) of Methodists in London are 65 or over and almost as many (46%) of United Reformed churchgoers, whereas only 8% of Pentecostals are in this age bracket, and only 11% of those going to New Churches. Outside these four denominations, all the others are similar in age structure (unlike in England as a whole) [Table 4.11].

However, it should be noted the Anglicans, Roman Catholics, Orthodox and Smaller denominations all have an average age above the overall of 41, and, because these four denominations account for half of the total attendance [Table 3.3], the inevitable result is that numbers are likely to decline rather than continue to increase over the next seven years [Table 3.3]. A fifth (21%) of London's churchgoers are in their Third Age or older.

As most Pentecostals are Charismatic Evangelicals, the average age of the latter (35) is similar to the average age of Pentecostals (33) [Table 4.13].

Six Outer London Boroughs have more than 25% of their attenders 65 or over [Figure 4.16], giving them a higher average age. The youngest Boroughs are Islington, Harrow and Waltham Forest, all with an average age of 35.

There are, thus, at least three challenges arising from this analysis:

- Why are there more young men than young women in church in London?
- What are the key features of the larger churches which so successfully attract those in their 20s?
- Can practical action be taken to prevent the seemingly inevitable decline of the older congregations?

5

Churches and their Leadership

This chapter examines the earlier questions on the Census form, such as the year the congregation started, the number of leaders and other staff, the number of services and so on, to give a picture of London church life in all its multitudinous variety. We begin with the year a church started.

Year congregation started

A few of London's churches still in use – some 3% – pre-date William the Conqueror's invasion of 1066, a smaller percentage than across England where it is 6%,[52] reflecting the larger rural population a millennium ago. The two centuries following the Conquest saw a huge church building programme as the population grew, and people settled into villages, feeling safe from Viking invasion as William built castles as well as churches. There was also a feudal system so the local lord could demand help in building a church, often so that people could pray for his soul. A sixth of all the churches in use in the country today were built in this period.

However, fewer churches were built then in London (just 5% of current churches were built between 1066 and 1699, against 20% in England as a whole), as, though a recognisable place where many lived, London had yet to become a metropolis. That began with industrialisation in the later eighteenth century (another 3% of London's churches were built then), and, mimicking the rest of Britain, there was a huge spurt in the nineteenth century, with a third (31%) of London's present churches being completed.

The capital saw many churches constructed in the early twentieth century, but the heavy bombing during World War

II meant church rebuilding became perhaps a greater priority than building. One such church, All Saint's in Plumstead, was rebuilt and opened in 1956 with a packed congregation, but it was rarely filled subsequently (although its fiftieth anniversary service in 2006 with Bishop Christopher Chessun presiding drew a congregation of over 250).

The dates London's churches were built are shown in Figure 5.1, illustrating the huge expansion in the last two centuries. The figures for the twenty-first century are based on just 12 years:

Figure 5.1: Number of churches still in use built in London per century since the 7th century

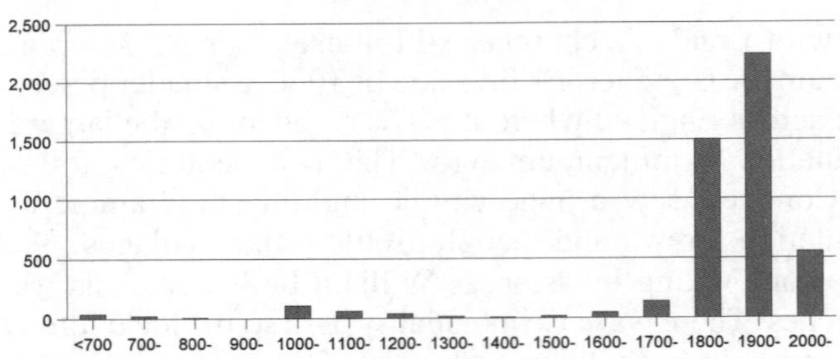

More recent congregational starts

One of the motives behind the 2012 London Church Census was to look at the way churches have been started – or planted – in the last 20 years. This is examined in more detail in a later chapter, but Figure 5.2 shows the number of churches or congregations started in each decade of the twentieth century and first ten years of the twenty-first; the impact of the two world wars is obvious.

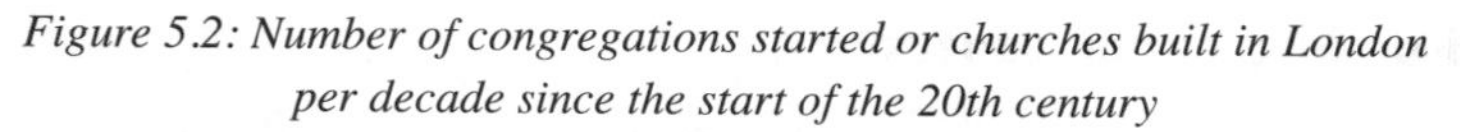

Figure 5.2: Number of congregations started or churches built in London per decade since the start of the 20th century

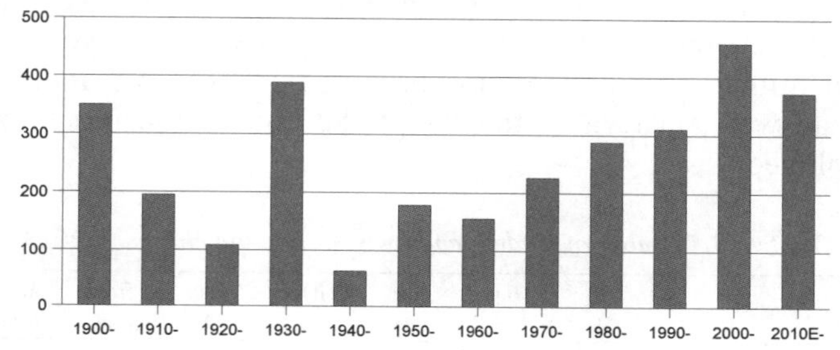

The increasing number of congregations founded every decade of the last half of the twentieth century may be clearly seen, and continues into the beginning of the present century (with the number shown for 2010 being an estimate based on the number started between 2010 and July 2012). It is a smaller number in line with the decreasing attendance already foreshadowed in Chapter 3.

Of the churches started between 2000 and 2009, two-fifths (37%) were Pentecostal and a quarter (24%) Independent, proportions similar to new congregations started between 1990 and 1999 (30% and 24% respectively).

Responsible for more than one church?

Was the minister or leader responsible for more than one church? One in 14, just 7%, were, a much smaller percentage than across England generally (32% in 2005[53]). Perhaps predictably, those looking after more than one church in London were either Methodist (36%), Pentecostal (28%), URC (13%), Smaller denominations (9%), Roman Catholic (7%) or Anglican (4%), with the other denominations not featuring.

The average number looked after was between two and three for each denomination except the Pentecostals where the average was five churches. Overall, in England, in 2005 the average was 2.9.

Employment of leaders

How many paid full-time (ordained and non-ordained) staff did the church employ and how many were employed part-time (either ordained or non-ordained)? Table 5.3 indicates the answers. Naturally, the larger the church the more were employed.

Table 5.3: Number of leaders employed in London churches, 2012

Number	None %	One %	Two %	Three %	Four %	Five or more %	Average number
Full-time ordained	*33*	*48*	*15*	*3*	*<–1–>*		0.9
Full-time non-ordained	*78*	*12*	*6*	*1*	*1*	*2*	0.4
Part-time, ord or non-ord.	*51*	*18*	*14*	*8*	*4*	*5*	1.2

Two-thirds (67%) of the churches had a paid ordained leader, a fifth (22%) had a paid non-ordained leader, with 11% having no paid leader. Half (49%) the churches, however, employed someone part-time (as well as any full-time person). These percentages did not vary significantly by denomination. While some of the unpaid leadership may be full-time, more likely it will be part-time, since many leaders, especially Pentecostal ministers, have a full-time paid job and then serve their church unpaid.

Youth Workers

"Does your church have a paid youth worker?""Yes, full-time," replied 7% of churches, and "Yes, part-time," said 6% of churches, meaning that seven churches out of eight (87%) in the capital did not employ a youth worker.

This is a much lower percentage than in the 1998 Census, when 21% of churches in England had a full-time paid youth worker.[54] Either it means here is another example of London's churches differing from others, or that the number of churches with youth workers has decreased considerably in the past 14 years; that the numbers of young people attending church have continued to decrease could mean the latter. The proportions with a youth worker are shown in Figure 5.4, New Churches and Anglicans having the most, the Orthodox and URC the least.

Figure 5.4: London churches with a youth worker by denomination, 2012

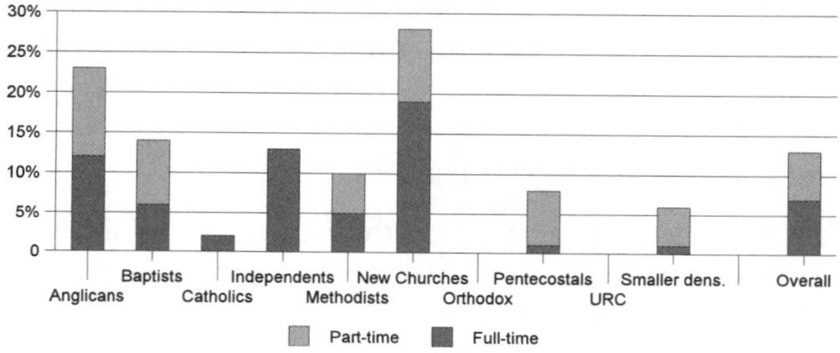

30%
25%
20%
15%
10%
5%
0
Anglicans
Baptists
Catholics
Independents
Methodists
New Churches
Orthodox
Pentecostals
URC
Smaller dens.
Overall
Part-time
Full-time

Year of appointment

When was the minister appointed? Almost two-fifths (37%) within the last five years, since 2008, and a further quarter (27%) in the five years before that, since 2003. One in every six, 17%, has served between 10 and 14 years, since 1998, and 8% were appointed between 1993 and 1997, 15 to 19 years ago. That means that one in every nine, 11%, have served for 20 years or longer. As Figure 5.5 makes clear this is somewhat different from England generally.[55]

Figure 5.5: Length of service of ministers, in England and London, 1998-2012

50%
40%
30%
20%
10%
0
Up to 5 years
6 to 10 years
11 to 15 years
Over 15 years
1998 England
2005 England
2012 London

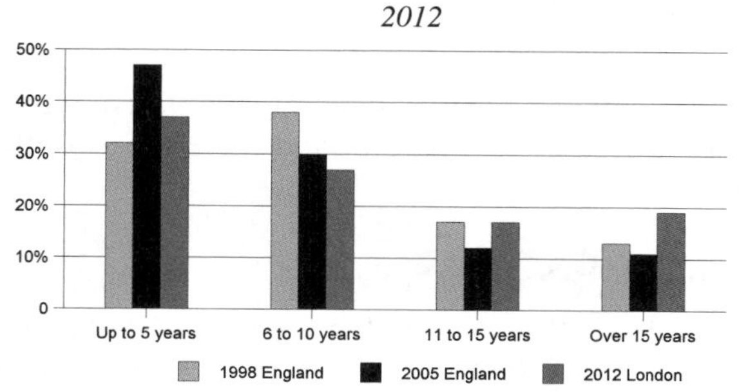

Whereas the average length of service decreased in England between 1998 and 2005 (from eight years to seven years) and has probably shortened slightly since, in London the average length of ministry at the time of the Census was eight years:

probably because leaders in larger churches are more likely to stay longer than in smaller churches, and because leaders of Independent churches especially are likely to stay longer than in other denominations.[56] Yet, these two factors at most account for only 25% of churches, so other influences may also be important.

Gender and age of church leaders

The question on the form asked the age-group of the minister of the church with the word "senior" being put in brackets as a number of London churches have several ministers, and, for these, the question was directed to the leader with overall responsibility. One church leader in six, 17%, was female, an identical percentage to churches across the UK in 2010.[57] It was highest in URC churches (50%), Smaller denominational churches (27%) and Methodist churches (25%).

Correlating with the fact that London ministers tend to stay longer in post was that rather more were 60 or over than in the country as a whole (29% to 23%), but their average age was the same at 54. A tenth, 10%, were under 40, a quarter (24%) were in their 40s, almost two-fifths (37%) were in their 50s, a fifth (22%) in their 60s and 7% were 70 or over in 2012. (See also Table 7.2)

A breakdown by denomination is given in Table A8. Baptists, New Churches and the Smaller denominational churches had the youngest ministers on average, and the Roman Catholics and Orthodox the oldest.

Frequency of services

The vast majority, 98%, of London's churches hold services weekly or more often. Just 1% hold them fortnightly, and 1% once a month. The large majority of these, 97%, are held on a Sunday, with 1% each being held on Wednesdays, Fridays or (collectively) the other days of the week. Some of the midweek services will be Bible Classes.

The number of services held on a Sunday is shown in Table 5.6:

Table 5.6: Number of services held on a Sunday

One	Two	Three	Four	Five or more	Average
48%	33%	11%	5%	3%	1.8

The Roman Catholic churches are by far the most likely to hold five or more services – a third (31%) have multiple Masses on a Sunday. Just 2% of Anglican churches have so many, and no other denomination has this number.

Frequency of attendance

How often did people attend services? The question was also asked across England in 1998 and 2005 and these answers are also given in Table 5.7:[58]

Table 5.7: Frequency of attending services in England and London, 1998-2012

Frequency	England 1998 %	England 2005 %	**London 2012 %**
Twice weekly	*15*	*18*	***12***
Weekly	*59*	*65*	***70***
Fortnightly	*14*	*11*	***12***
Monthly	*12*	*6*	***6***

The frequency of London's churchgoers is much the same as elsewhere, with the majority, over two-thirds, going to church weekly, with a few going more frequently and the rest less. In 2005, it was especially those aged 30 to 44 who went less frequently, but this was not measured in the London Census.

Visitors

In addition to regular attenders, the Census form asked if a person was a visitor. One in 16, 6%, said they were, a percentage which compares with 5% across England in both 1998 and 2005. London's churches could conceivably be expected to have more visitors; certainly the larger churches will have many; in a 1981 congregational survey of All Souls, Langham Place, 36% were visitors![59]

Attendance at extra times

I once sat in front of a couple at a crowded carol service, and, not recognising them, introduced myself and asked if they had been before. "Oh," they replied, "we come regularly," which I took to mean coming every week, or maybe every month. I apologised for not knowing them and asked when they had started coming. "We had a tragedy in our family," they said, "our 22-year old son was killed three years ago in an accident. The church did such a wonderful funeral for him that we come every Christmas to say 'thank you' and to remember him."

Clearly, "regularity" is defined in the eyes of the beholder! There are, however, many people who come occasionally to church, many more than attend on a weekly basis. The Census form asked for such numbers to be estimated. They showed, over the course of a year, the number of people who come less often than monthly is more than double the number who come on a Sunday. Sunday worshippers, although mostly coming every week, are but a third (31%) of the total footfall in London's churches across a year. The potential for outreach is great.

Of these extra people,

- 6% come quarterly
- 26%, a quarter, come twice a year, and
- 68%, two-thirds, come just at Christmas.

This last is an extraordinary percentage, which, if only approximately correct, would suggest that an extra 1.6 million people attend church at Christmas in London. If all these actually lived in London, that would be an extra fifth, 20%, of the population. That is, in addition, to the 9% already attending regularly (defined as at least once a month).

A further point of interest: in 2012, Anglicans were 12% of the usual churchgoers in London (Table 3.3), but at Christmas they account for over 80% of the extra people coming to church, thus giving the Anglican church a huge challenge and enormous opportunity. This percentage is double that of Christmas attendance across England.

Ethnicity

London's churchgoers are obviously a complete ethnic mix. Into what groups do they actually fall? Unlike the Population Census, the London Census did not break down the Black component into African, Caribbean or any other, but it did partially divide the Asian component. Details are given in Table 5.8:

Table 5.8: Ethnic groups of London churchgoers, 2012

Group:	White %	Black %	Asian %	Mixed %	Other %	Asian I/P/B %	Asian C/J/K %	Asian Other %	Base (=100%)
Churchgoers	***53***	***28***	***12***	***5***	***2***	***6***	***3***	***3***	**0.7 m**
Population	*60*	*13*	*18*	*6*	*3*	*6*	*1*	*5*	8.2 m
Ch'goers as % of population	***8***	***19***	***8***	***8***	***5***	***4***	***16***	***6***	***9***

I/P/B = Indian, Pakistani and Bangladeshi. C/J/K = Chinese., Japanese and Korean

Almost a fifth (19%) of the Black population in London goes to church, a huge percentage, confirming the importance of religion in the life of the Black community, and the cultural dominance of the spiritual in the thinking and background of many. A sixth (16%) of the Chinese, Japanese and Korean community also go, illustrating the important work of these churches in the capital. The Japanese work is less strong, almost fading in the 1990s, but is now recovering with several congregations.

Given that many of those from the Indian sub-continent will be Muslims, it is not surprising their church attendance is the lowest of London's population at 4%.

Trend over time

Table 5.9 shows how these figures compare with earlier years; the "mixed" category was only introduced in 2012, and is included in this Table with "Black" since many are half-Black.

Table 5.9: Ethnicity of churchgoers in London, 1998-2020E

Year	White %	Black %	Asian %	Other %	Asian I/P/B %	Asian C/J/K %	Asian Other %	Base (=100%)
1998	*64*	*24*	*10*	*2*	*4*	*3*	*3*	617,900
2005	*57*	*29*	*12*	*2*	*5*	*3*	*4*	623,000
2012	*53*	*33*	*12*	*2*	*6*	*3*	*3*	**721,500**
2020E	*47*	*38*	*13*	*2*	*7*	*3*	*3*	704,100

The Table clearly shows the decreasing proportion of white churchgoers in London and the fast increasing proportion of Black. Asians and others remain roughly the same percentage – about one in every seven, though those from the Indian sub-continent are growing (largely because of Roman Catholic influence). If the trend suggested continues, then, by 2020, whites will be in a minority throughout the city's churches with the Blacks being very numerous (though concentrated much more in particular congregations).

Variation by denomination

Table A9 in the Appendix breaks down the 2012 figures by denomination, and these figures are illustrated in Figure 5.10. The chart shows Orthodox churches are attended almost entirely (96%) by white people, although in this case mostly non-British white people, coming mainly from European countries.

Figure 5.10: Ethnicity of London's churchgoers, by denomination, 2012

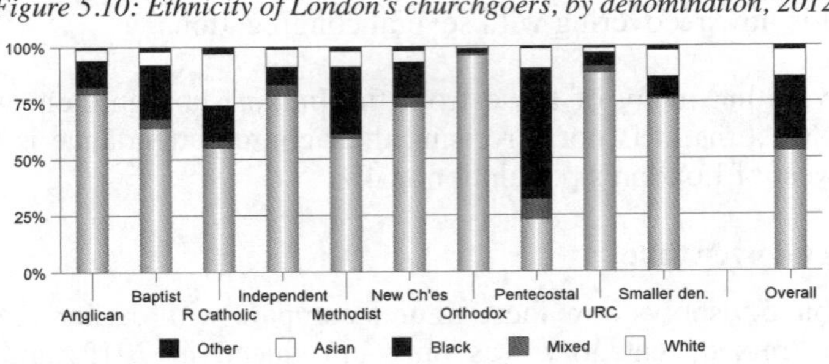

The United Reformed Church has the next highest percentage of white people, five-sixths (88%), followed by Black (6%) then others (6%). Anglicans (79%), Independents (78%), New Churches (73%) and the Smaller denominations (76%) are all about three-quarters white, with Black the next largest group for Anglicans and New Churches. Yet Asians are equally with Blacks for Independent churches (8% each) and more than Blacks for the Smaller denominations (12% to 9%).

Baptists (64%), Roman Catholics (55%) and Methodists (59%) are all about three-fifths attended by white people, with Blacks making up the difference in Baptist and Methodist congregations, and Asians (especially those from the Indian sub-continent) in the Roman Catholics. Not all Methodist churches belong to the Methodist Church of Great Britain; a strong Methodist emphasis exists in a number of Black denominations; reflected here in the 30% of Methodists who are Black.

The Pentecostals differ most from the other denominations. Almost three-fifths of their attenders (58%) are Black, followed by whites (23%), and then almost equally Asians and others. It simply proves the Pentecostal growth is driven by the Black Majority Churches (BMCs).

Variation by size of church

Details of ethnicity by size of church are given in Table A10 in the Appendix, but the proportions of each ethnic group do not vary significantly by church size. The proportion of whites is higher in smaller churches than larger ones (59% to 50%), but this is partly because the Roman Catholics, who tend to have much larger churches than others, have an exceptional number of Asians in their congregations, especially from the Indian sub-continent, which affects the proportion of others in larger churches. Black people are less proportionately in larger congregations than smaller (28% to 33%), and Asians are especially numerous in congregations of between 50 and 100 and the largest churches.

Variation by location

Thus, as we have seen before in other Census questions, denomination is the key discriminating factor for ethnicity, together with location – white churchgoers are far fewer in Inner London than Outer London as Figure 5.11 shows. Black churchgoers in Inner London are now virtually half (48%) of the overall total. In Outer London they are a fifth (21%).

Figure 5.11: Attendance by ethnicity

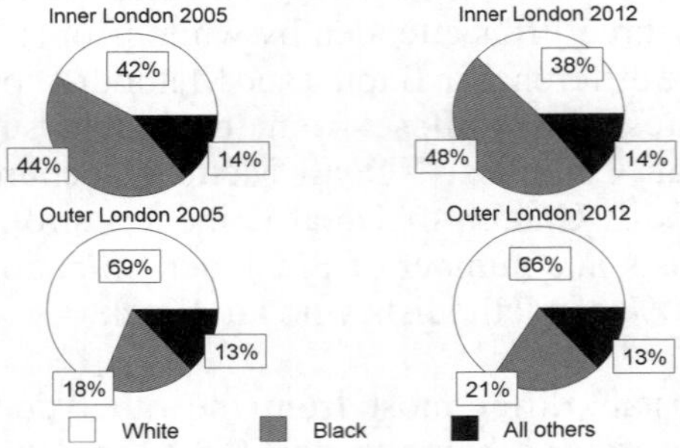

Inner London 2005
42%
44%
14%
Inner London 2012
38%
48%
14%
Outer London 2005
69%
18%
13%
Outer London 2012
66%
21%
13%
White
Black
All others

The influx of immigrants has increased the proportion of Black attenders in Inner London. It should be noted that, generally, black Africans are increasingly moving out of London to other parts of Britain. In 2001, 80% of the black Africans in Britain lived in London; in 2011, just 58% did (probably following employment opportunities).[60]

Variation by churchmanship

Figure 5.12 shows the variations of ethnicity by churchmanship, and Table A11 in the Appendix gives the figures. The greatest percentages of white people are in Broad churches (74%), Liberal (70%), Broad Evangelical (66%), Mainstream Evangelical (66%) and Low Church (64%).

The greatest proportion of Black people are found in Charismatic Evangelical churches (virtually half, 48%), followed by Anglo-Catholics (35%) and Broad Evangelicals (25%). Catholics have a high proportion of Asians (21%, mostly from the Indian sub-continent) as do Other churchmanships (29%, all Chinese, Japanese or Korean). The latter is somewhat unexpected.

Figure 5.12: Ethnicity of London's churchgoers, by churchmanship, 2012

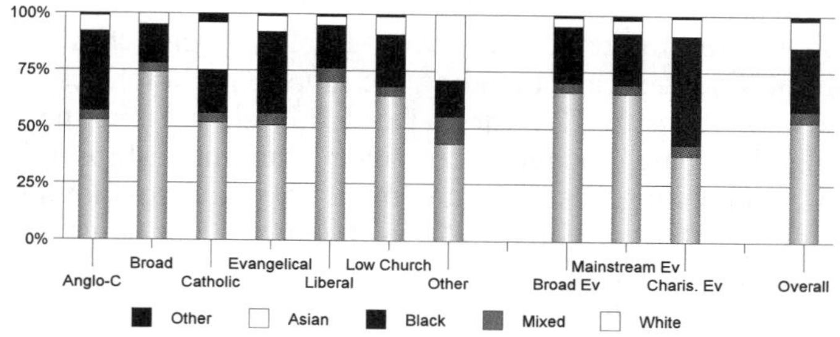

100%
75%
50%
25%
0%
Anglo-C
Broad
Catholic
Evangelical
Liberal
Low Church
Other
Mainstream Ev
Broad Ev
Charis. Ev
Overall
Other
Asian
Black
Mixed
White

Length of attendance at church

How long had people been attending that particular church? (The question was not asked in previous Censuses so comparison with earlier years unfortunately is not possible.) On average for 10 years, but the variation in answers is fairly even:

- 23% have been attending for up to three years
- 19% for between 3 and 5 years
- 21% for between 6 and 10 years
- 18% for between 11 and 20 years, and
- 19% for 20 years or more.

Figure 5.13: Average length of time people had been attending their current London church, 2012

15
10
5
0
Years
Anglican
Baptist
R Catholic
Independent
Methodist
New Churches
Orthodox
Pentecostal
URC
Smaller den
Overall

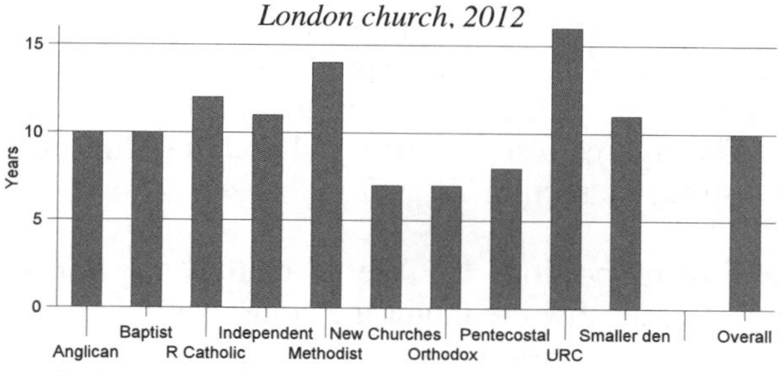

These varied somewhat by denomination, as given in detail in Table A12 in the Appendix, with the average times illustrated in Figure 5.13. The URC and Methodists have the longest attendance (16 and 14 years), which is twice as long as those attending New Churches, Orthodox or Pentecostal churches (7, 7 and 8 years respectively).Those in smaller churches (congregations of 50 or under) had been there slightly longer than those in larger churches (over 200) – 12 years to 10. Similarly, the figures did not vary greatly by churchmanship, with the Evangelicals attending their present church less than others (9 years to 12 years). Does this stem from the fact Evangelicals are younger than other churchmanships (Table 4.13), and younger people are more involved in moving in terms of houses and jobs, and less inclined to put down roots? Or is it because Evangelicals have seen more growth than some other churchmanships?

Distance from the church

This question was also not asked in previous Censuses. Respondents were asked to estimate how many of their congregation lived within half a mile, up to three miles or over three miles away from their church. The average distance, taking "over three miles" as five miles, was two miles, made up as follows:

- 32% lived within half a mile
- 44% lived between half a mile and 3 miles, and
- 24% lived more than 3 miles away.

These varied by denomination, with the Anglicans, Baptists, Roman Catholics and URC living closest to their churches, and the Methodists, Orthodox and Smaller denominations furthest away on average, with other denominations between these two groups. The figures also varied by churchmanship but not so greatly, as may be seen in Table 5.14.

The varying proportions by size of church are illustrated in Figure 5.15 and show the larger the congregation (up to 200 in size) an increasing proportion of a congregation live closer to the church, suggesting more successful evangelism takes place in the vicinity of a church and that while "specialist" churches are important, growth, perhaps, is more likely when based in the local context. The largest churches, however, have a greater proportion coming from three or more miles away, showing the eclectic nature of their congregations.

Table 5.14: Average distance London congregations lived from their church, 2012, in miles

Denomination	Dist	Churchmanship	Dist	Size of congregation	Dist
Anglican	1.9	Anglo-Catholic	1.5	Under 26	2.2
Baptist	1.8	Broad	1.9	26 to 50	2.1
Roman Catholic	1.5	Catholic	1.6	51 to 100	2.0
Independent	2.2	Broad Evangelical	1.8	101 to 200	1.9
Methodist	3.1	Mainstream Evan	2.1	Over 200	2.1
New Churches	2.2	Charismatic Evan	2.3		
Orthodox	3.7	Total evangelical	2.2		
Pentecostal	2.6	Liberal	2.3		
United Reformed	1.8	Low Church	1.9		
Smaller denoms.	3.0	All others	3.6	Overall	2.1

Figure 5.15: Distance lived from the church by size of congregations, 2012

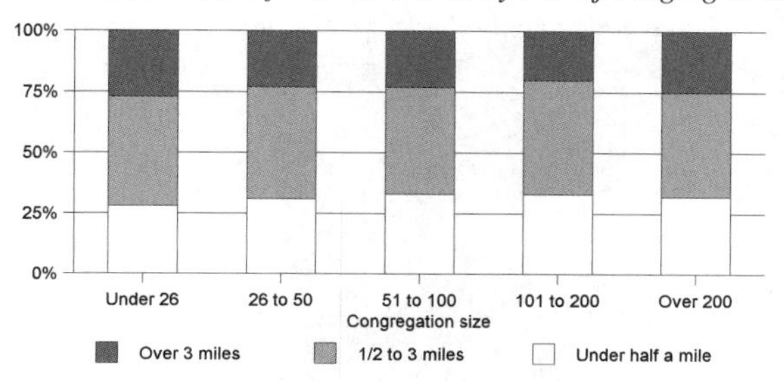

People travel, however, far shorter distances to church in Outer London than in Inner, where the average respective distances are 1.8 and 2.4 miles: this shows the eclectic nature of the capital's central church life, both larger churches and "specialist" churches (often using a language other than English) illustrating the advantage of ease of travelling in Inner London on Sundays. Figures 5.16 and 5.17 show the variations of percentages for the lower and higher bounds of travel.

Figure 5.16: Percentage of churchgoers travelling under half a mile to church

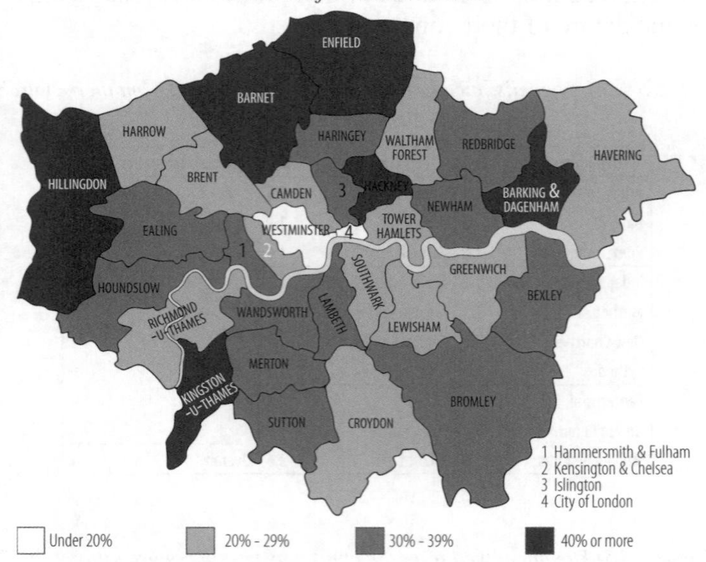

Figure 5.17: Percentage of churchgoers travelling 3 miles or more to church

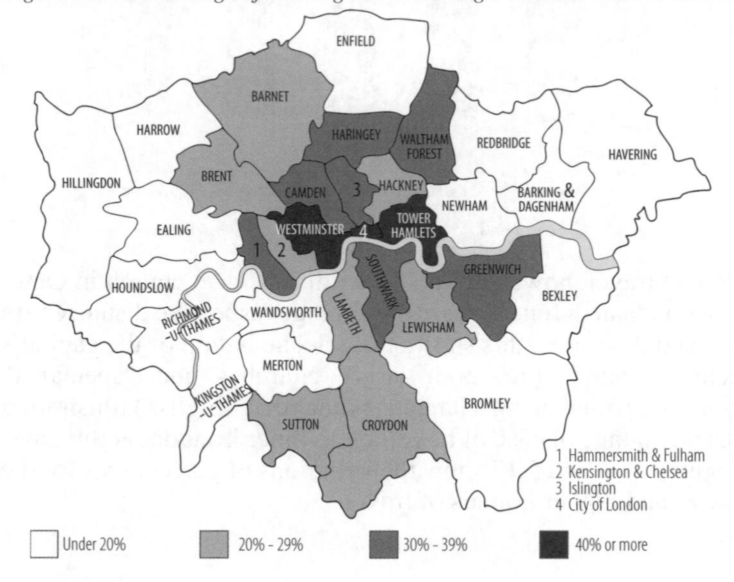

So what does all this say?

This Chapter has looked at leaders and the people coming to their churches. The large majority of churches in London were built in the nineteenth and twentieth centuries, and, in particular, an increasing number of congregations have been started every decade since the 1960s until we get to the current decade when the number of new starts is forecast to be lower than in the last.

Just 7% of ministers serving in London were responsible for more than one church, a much smaller percentage than England generally (32%). Most of these were responsible for just a further one or two churches. Two-fifths (37%) were appointed within the last five years, and a further quarter (27%) in the five years before that. However, there are more ministers serving for 15 years or more in their present church than in England generally, partly because those in larger churches tend to stay for longer.

Two-thirds of churches (67%) had a paid ordained leader, and a fifth (22%) a paid non-ordained leader. Half (49%) employed a leader part-time. One church in eight, 13%, had a full-time or part-time paid youth leader; a percentage much smaller than the 1998 national figure (21%).

Half (48%) of the city's churches have a single service on Sundays, and third (33%) have two. Roman Catholics are most likely to have multiple services on a Sunday.

Two-thirds of London churchgoers (70%) attend every week, with most of the rest either coming more often or once a fortnight. A substantial number, however, come less frequently, mostly either twice a year or just at Christmas. The extra numbers coming at Christmas are very large, amounting to perhaps a fifth, 20%, of London's population, the great majority of whom attend Anglican churches.

Half (53%) of London's churchgoers are white, and just over a quarter (28%) are Black, quite different percentages to the general population (60% and 13% respectively). One black person in five (19%) goes to church, compared with 8% of white people. One Chinese, Japanese, or Korean in six (16%) also attends. The proportion of whites has been decreasing since 1998; it is forecast to decline further.

In Inner London, however, white people make up only 38% of the churchgoers, against almost half (48%) black. In Outer London the percentages are 66%, and 21%, respectively. The largest proportion of black churchgoers are Pentecostal; two-thirds (66%) of all black worshippers, though some may be found in every denomination (and churchmanship). Roman Catholics have an especially large number of attenders from the Indian sub-continent, probably with a substantial amount coming from Goa, India's smallest state by area.

On average, London's churchgoers have been attending the same church for 10 years, though in some denominations (URC and Methodists especially), average length is longer (16 and 14 years respectively).

A third (32%) of those attending church in London are within half a mile of where they live, almost half (44%) between half and three miles away, while the remaining quarter (24%) travel more than three miles. Those living in Inner London travel more than those in Outer London (2.4 miles to 1.8 miles respectively). Intriguingly, the larger the church the greater the proportion of people coming who live close to it, except for the very largest churches.

6

Church Activities

This Chapter looks at the questions which were grouped into two blocks: Questions 16 to 18 on Mid-week activities, and Questions 19 to 21 on other Church Activities.

Mid-week Worship

Did churches have regular mid-week worship, such as a communion service, Mass, or a "Bible Class" teaching (or preaching) opportunity? Just over three-fifths, 63%, of London's churches did, a percentage varying by denomination as shown in Figure 6.1:

Figure 6.1: Percentage of London's churches holding mid-week worship services, 2012

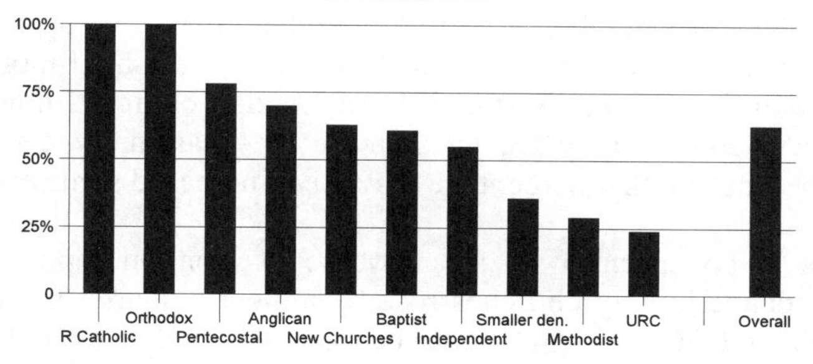

All the Orthodox and Roman Catholic churches responding held mid-week services, followed by three-quarters (77%) of the Pentecostals, then two-thirds of the Anglicans (69%). Churches with fewest mid-week worship events were the URC (24%) and Methodists (29%).

The detail by individual Borough is given in *Church Statistics*, but there are more churches holding mid-week services in Inner London than Outer London (65% to 61%). In both 1998 and 2005, two-fifths, 42%, of churches nationally had a mid-week service, but the specific percentage held in those years in London's churches is unknown.[61]

The larger the church the more likely it was to hold mid-week services: half (49%) of the churches in the capital with 25 or fewer people in their congregation had such a service, rising to over three-quarters (78%) for the larger churches (congregations of 200 or more).

Number attending mid-week

In total, the number attending mid-week worship services in London in 2012 was 164,900, or 23% of Sunday attendance;[62] comparing with 9% nationally in 1998, and 15% nationally in 2005. Either mid-week attendance in London has increased significantly since 2005 or, in yet another aspect of church life, London contrasts with the rest of the country. The average attendance is 55 people.

Given the huge workforce in central London during the week, and the large number of active churches, it is not surprising mid-week services, such as lunch hour ones, are held more in London than generally (the 63% of London churches holding them is considerably greater than the 42% nationally, even if, in the interim, that percentage may have increased somewhat).

This is consistent with the Diocese of London report that attendance in City churches rose by almost a quarter between 2008 and 2012. Former Archdeacon of London, Ven Peter Delaney, told *The Financial Times* "stress and anxiety were causing financial workers to seek comfort in the Christian faith". Many city workers were questioning their values, reported a churchwarden, James Gerry, of St Mary Woolnoth.[63]

Anglicans have specifically measured mid-week service attendance nationally since the year 2000, churches and cathedrals separately. In their churches, attendance is about 13% of Sunday attendance but it has remained level over the last 10 years, while Sunday attendance has fallen. Cathedral mid-week attendance, on the other hand, has rapidly increased over the last decade from about a third of Sunday attendance to almost two-thirds.[64]

Of those attending mid-week in London, 45% are male and 55% female, echoing the 44% and 56% attending on a Sunday.

Age of those attending mid-week

The questionnaire didn't ask for much detail about age of mid-week attenders, but the basic information provided is given in Table 6.2. The dominance of young men under 20 over women attending mid-week is exceedingly clear, again implying that many of these probably sing in choirs, even though it is common for choirs to also have girl choristers nowadays.

Table 6.2: Age of those attending mid-week services in London, 2012

Age-group	Under 20[1] %	20 to 44 %	45 to 64 %	65 & over[2] %	Average age	Base (=100%)
Male	25	33	26	16	42	74,800
Female	14	36	28	22	47	90,100
Total	19	35	27	19	44	164,900

[1] Taken as 12 for the average [2] Taken as 75 for the average

Mid-week attenders are slightly older on average than Sunday attenders, by about five years. This is because rather more of those aged 20 to 44 and 45 to 64 attend mid-week than on a Sunday (18% and 20% respectively) and fewer of those aged under 20 (12%) or who are 65 or over (15%).

The concentration of those aged 20 to 44 attending a mid-week church service is not unique to church activities. As Tony Travers of the London School of Economics points out, "the capital exerts a magnetic pull on ambitious career-makers from across the country".[65] In 2010, 19% of England's local councillors were under 50; in London the proportion was 33%.

By size of church

Exactly half of those coming mid-week (50%) attend a church with a large congregation on a Sunday (200 or over) in contrast to three-fifths (58%) of Sunday worshippers who attend a large church: showing churches with less than 200 are also very active mid-week. This is especially true for churches with between 100 and 200 on a Sunday, as their mid-week attendance amounts to a quarter (25%) of the total whereas their Sunday worship only accounts for a fifth (20%) of churchgoers.

By denomination

Table 6.3 shows the number attending mid-week by denomination, and their percentage of the total. The third line, taken from Table 3.3, shows the percentage attending on a Sunday which may be compared with the percentages in the second line. They demonstrate Anglican, Baptist, Independent churches and those belonging to the Smaller denominations are especially active mid-week.

Table 6.3: Numbers attending mid-week, their percentage of the total, and average attendance, 2012

Denomination	Anglican	Baptist	Roman Catholic	Independent	Methodist	New	Orthodox	Pentecostal	URC	Smaller Denoms	Total
Mid-week number	40,400	15,700	26,400	10,100	3,900	9,900	3,400	42,700	1,000	14,000	164,900
As % of total	*25*	*9*	*14*	*6*	*2*	*6*	*2*	*26*	*1*	*9*	*100*
Sunday total % [T 3.3]	*12*	*6*	*27*	*4*	*2*	*6*	*3*	*32*	*1*	*7*	*100*
Average mid-week attendance	57	70	62	55	54	48	44	37	28	78	55

The last line in the Table gives the average attendance at each church. While overall this is 55 per church (which may be spread across more than one service mid-week, the number held not asked), it is highest for the mid-week services held in the Smaller denominations, followed by the Baptists and Roman

Catholics, and lowest for the URC, Pentecostal and Orthodox denominations.

By churchmanship

Some Evangelical churches in particular promote their lunch-time services for workers. Three-fifths (62%) of those attending such mid-week events in churches are in Evangelical churches, about the same proportion as attend on a Sunday (61%, Table 1.11). Their average attendance is 57, very similar to that of non-Evangelical churches, which average 52.

By location

Numbers attending mid-week services are greater in Inner London than Outer London. Three-fifths (60%) of mid-week attenders are in Inner London. Of the 98,700 attending in Inner London, a quarter (24%) attend services in the several very sizeable churches across the City of London, of the order of 23,000 people every week, of whom the vast majority, 90%, are aged between 20 and 44. A few of these churches only offer mid-week services.

A further 10% of Inner London mid-weekers attend services in the City of Westminster, some 10,300 people, though these are spread more evenly across the different age groups.

By Sunday attendance

Respondents were asked to estimate how many of those coming each week also attended a Sunday service (though this might not necessarily be at the same church). Just over half (54%) said they all did, and the average of the remaining responses was 69%, two-thirds. Combined with the 54%, the average would be 86%.

This percentage did not vary significantly by size of church, nor between Inner and Outer London,[66] but it did differ by denomination. The Anglicans were the lowest, at 77%, suggesting there was more non-Sunday attenders in their mid-week services than in other denominations.

If 86% of those coming to mid-week services also attended church on a Sunday, that means that 14% do not. That means an extra 23,100 people across London additionally come to church during the week, or an extra 4% to those already attending, making the grand weekly attendance 744,600 or 9% of the total population.

These extra people come from a total of 333,700 attend church weekly in Inner London and 410,900 in Outer London, respectively 10.3% and 8.3% of the actual populations. While these extra numbers are important, they need to be looked at in the context of total attendance, which Figure 6.4 seeks to do:

Figure 6.4: Sunday and mid-week attendance, Inner and Outer London, 2012

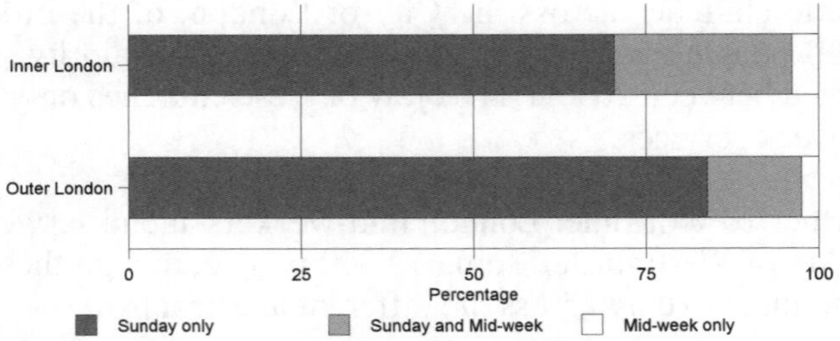

Inner London
Outer London
0 25 50 75 100
Percentage
Sunday only
Sunday and Mid-week
Mid-week only

Young people's activities

Did the young people in a respondent's church attend a regular youth activity such as a youth club or something similar? Slightly under half, 45%, of respondents said they did. This compares with 27% of churches nationally (in 2005) and 47% of Scottish churches (in 2002),[67] suggesting perhaps that churches in London have more resources than others, or that more and more churches recognise the importance of having something specifically for young people.

New Churches, Independent and Pentecostal churches were most likely to have such activities (62%, 56% and 52% respectively), while the Orthodox, URC and Methodists were least likely (20%, 24% and 36% respectively).

"Resources" in this context may not be just having adequate premises or space, nor the necessary financial backing, but the need to have people who are capable of, and available for, running such youth work. We have seen that only 13% of London's churches employ a part-time or full-time youth worker, and it is the New Churches and Independent churches which have the highest percentage of these (Figure 5.4). They presumably would hold such activities. The larger churches (100 or more in the congregation) were more likely to have youth work than smaller churches (60% to 35%), probably because of the greater availability of suitable volunteers.

Number attending

The youth activities attracted, on average, 30 people under the age of 19 per church, which is virtually the same as the national figure of 31 in 2005. The larger churches (100 or more) had on average twice as many young people attending mid-week activities than smaller churches (44 to 19). This gives a total across London of 64,700 young people.

The Anglican churches in the capital had the largest average number of young people (51, a similar number to those attending nationally in 2005), but the Anglicans have a number of sizeable churches in London, some of which have especially high numbers of young people, which boosts the overall average. As many of these are Inner London churches, this is also reflected in the fact that the Inner London average is slightly higher than the Outer London average (33 to 29 young people).

After the Anglicans, the Roman Catholics and Smaller denominations had the highest number of young people on average per church – in this case, it was the same at 23 each. Baptists and Independents averaged 17, New Churches 15, Pentecostal churches 13, and Methodists and URC 10 (in the churches which had any young people attending activities at all). The average over all churches in a particular denomination would be just under half these figures.

Sunday attendance

Respondents were also asked to estimate what percentage of the young people attending mid-week went to church on Sunday. The overall average was 76%. Totalling the number of young people attending mid-week per church, the percentage of churches with young people's activities, and the number of churches in London, gives a figure of about 49,200 young people attending mid-week activities who also attend on a Sunday, leaving 15,500 attending only mid-week. Perhaps as many young people who already come to church across London on a Sunday might attend a youth activity mid-week if there was one. In other words, of young people coming to church in London, half attend something specifically for them and half do not or cannot. Could this mean there is scope for more churches to undertake youth work if the resources and opportunity were there?

Attendance at non-worship activities

The Census form also asked for estimates of the number of people attending mid-week church activities, such as Drop-in Centres or Lunch Clubs, who do not normally attend worship services at any church. Outside organisations which might hire rooms or make use of church premises were to be excluded.

London churches had an average of 71 people attending mid-week community-type activities but not a Sunday service, a total of some 78,200 people. This is a fifth (19%) of the total number attending such across England as a whole in 2005, a larger percentage than the 12% of England's churches located in London in 2012, reflecting the greater ease and awareness of suburban or urban community activity.

The percentage of men attending non-worship activites was 39%, similar to the 37% nationally in 2005, but much smaller than the 44% of men attending church on a Sunday. Figure 6.5 shows their breakdown by age, also comparing Sunday attendance and national attendance.

Figure 6.5: Age of those going to mid-week church-run activities and Sunday attendance, 2012

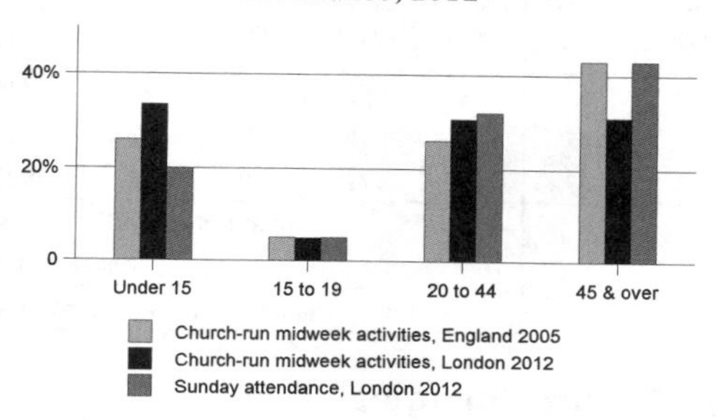

Comparing the first two columns of Figure 6.5 shows London has a higher percentage of children than across England generally coming to mid-week activities. Figure 6.5 indicates about the same proportion of people coming between ages 15 and 44, but far fewer older people, aged 45 or more; consistent with the percentages in Table 4.4.

The last two columns of Figure 6.5 show that in London a greater proportion of children came to mid-week activities than come to church on a Sunday, and a smaller proportion of older people. In other words, mid-week activities are great for encouraging children to come to church-run events, so the challenge, therefore, is helping more churches to run these.

Combining total mid-week attendance

Table 6.6 summarises the figures given for the various kinds of mid-week activities in this Chapter.

The overall total of people involved with church in London is a fraction over 10% of the overall population (10.1%), of whom 14% come only mid-week, 23% come both mid-week and on a Sunday, and just over three-fifths (63%) come only on a Sunday.

Table 6.6: Mid-week activities by type in total

Mid-week activity	% of churches having this		Average attendance		% attending on a Sunday		Total mid-week attendance London 2012	Of whom attending midweek only 2012
	England 2005	London 2012	England 2005	London 2012	England 2005	London 2012		
Services	*42*	***63***	*29*	***55***	*72*	***86***	164,900	**23,100**
Youth	*27*	***45***	*31*	***30***	*45*	***76***	64,700	**15,500**
Church-run	*20*	***23***	*55*	***71***	*0*	***0***	78,200	**78,200**
			TOTAL midweek 2012				307,800	**116,800**
			Sunday attendance					**721,500**
			Total attendance Sunday and mid-week					**838,300**

Ownership of church building

"Is the building in which you meet borrowed, hired, rented or owned by the church?" was not asked in previous Censuses, but, in keeping with the innovatory inclination to start new congregations, a fifth (21%) of churches in London are rented, hired or share their worship building with another church. This percentage varied greatly by denomination, as Figure 6.7 shows, with New Churches and Pentecostal churches having three-fifths (63%) of their churches in rented or shared buildings. The more institutional denominations like the Anglicans, Roman Catholics, Methodist and URC had the lowest percentage of hired churches. The Orthodox percentage in Figure 6.7 is based on a tiny number of respondents and is, therefore, uncertain.

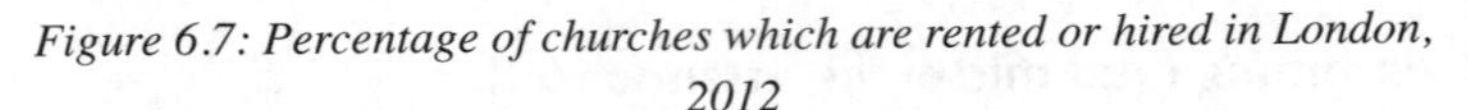
Figure 6.7: Percentage of churches which are rented or hired in London, 2012

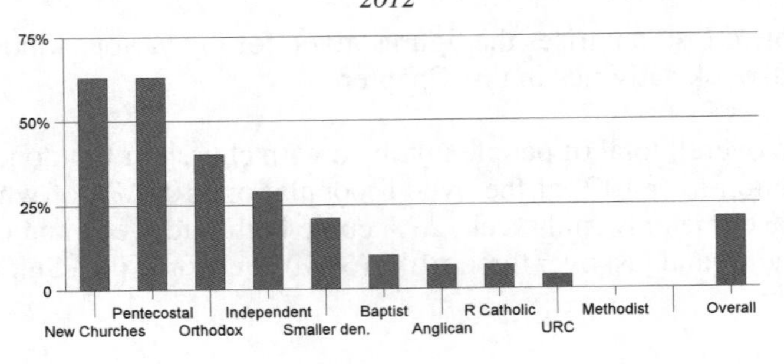

The smaller the church the more likely it was to be using a hired building (33% for the smallest churches – 25 or under – to 13% for the largest churches). The variation by Borough is given in a *Church Statistics*, but is illustrated in Figure 6.8.

Figure 6.8: Percentages of churches used hired or rented buildings, 2012

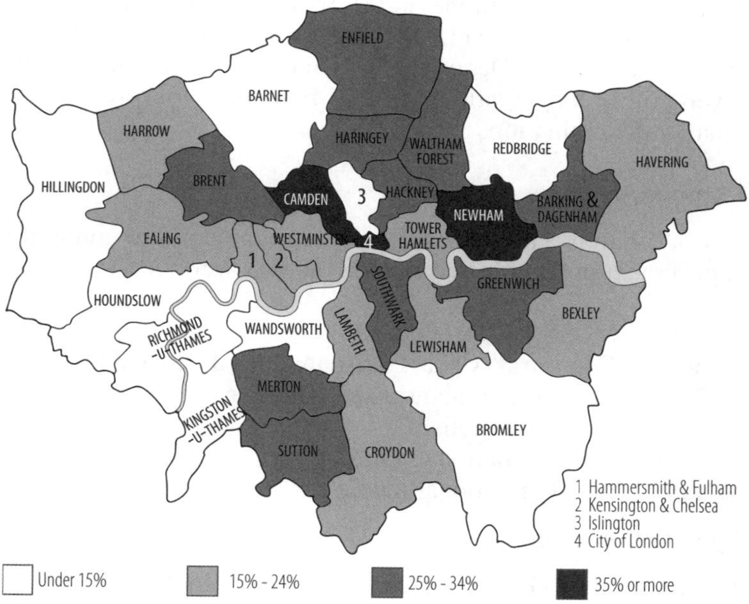

Length of rent

Did churches which rented or hired have use of the building for the whole of a Sunday or just part of it? A third (32%) had use of their building for the whole of Sunday and two-thirds (68%) for part of it. This did not vary by denomination, churchmanship or size of church.

Multiple use

Did other churches use the same building? Three-fifths (59%) said they had sole use, and two-fifths (41%) shared with other churches. A fifth (20%) shared it with one other church, a sixth

(17%) with two others and a small percentage (4%) with three or more, the overall average being two, if shared.

Across all London congregations, a small number have services in a building used by several congregations, while the majority do not share at all and one in five share with just one other church. The large churches (200 or more) are least likely to share at all, usually because they have multiple services of their own on a Sunday. Denominations most likely to share with several other congregations are the Methodists, followed by the Smaller denominations.

Community engagement

Did a church have an active programme of community engagement in six selected areas? Answers were:

- 73% Meeting social needs
- 54% Courses as Alpha, Christianity Explored and Emmaus
- 34% Regular neighbourhood visitation
- 33% Street evangelism
- 14% Local or national politics
- 11% Local or national media.

By churchmanship

These varied by churchmanship as shown in Table 6.9:

Table 6.9: Community engagement by churchmanship of London churches, 2012

Churchmanship	Anglo Cath %	Broad %	Catholic %	Evangelical Broad %	Evangelical Main. %	Evangelical Charis. %	Evangelical Total %	Liberal %	Low Church %	Others %	***Overall* %**
Meeting social needs	*89*	*69*	*89*	*82*	*65*	*69*	*68*	*85*	*67*	*67*	***73***
Teaching courses	*37*	*46*	*56*	*65*	*67*	*52*	*59*	*47*	*45*	*33*	***54***
Neighbourhood visitation	*26*	*35*	*58*	*29*	*34*	*37*	*35*	*27*	*27*	*20*	***34***
Street evangelism	*11*	*12*	*6*	*6*	*42*	*61*	*49*	*4*	*16*	*40*	***33***
Local/national politics	*32*	*12*	*14*	*24*	*6*	*10*	*9*	*21*	*13*	*0*	***14***
Local/national media	*5*	*12*	*3*	*18*	*6*	*13*	*11*	*16*	*10*	*0*	***11***
Base (=100%)	238	191	610	222	1,191	1,492	2,905	352	313	182	**4,791**

Main. = Mainstream Charis. = Charismatic

This Table shows some of the basic differences between the Broad/Liberal churches and the Evangelical ones, and between these and Catholic churches. Meeting social needs is strong for Catholics, Anglo-Catholics and Liberals, but weaker for all the other groups (88% to 68%). Holding teaching courses is strongest for Evangelicals and Catholics, but weaker for the other groups (58% to 42%).

Neighbourhood visitation is especially strong, almost double, for the Catholics compared with everyone else (58% to 30%). Street evangelism, on the other hand, is particularly conducted by the Charismatic, then the Mainstream Evangelicals (61% and 42%, and then 8% for all other groups).

Local and national politics is strongest for the Anglo-Catholics but weakest for the Evangelicals (32% to 9%) and the other groups. Local and national media are fairly low whatever the churchmanship.

The type of activities undertaken in any of these categories was not requested, but one respondent sent details of the Wandsworth African Caribbean Association with which she was associated, working from a local school. They were "people working for a better environment".[68]

By denomination

Table 6.10 gives the percentage of churches involved in these different community engagements by denomination: there is a wide variation, illustrated by the shaded squares indicating where a percentage is much above or below the average. Roman Catholics and Methodists are especially involved in meeting local social needs, while the Orthodox, Pentecostals and URC less so, although the Orthodox do much within their own community. Anglicans and the New Churches are more likely than average to hold teaching courses; Methodists, the Orthodox, Pentecostals, URC and Smaller denominations not as much, although the Orthodox do provide teaching but not through these ready-made courses.

Table 6.10: Community engagement by denomination of London churches, 2012

Denomination	Anglican %	Baptist %	R Catholic %	Independent %	Methodist %	New Chur's %	Orthodox %	Pentecostal %	URC %	Smaller dens. %	***Overall %***
Meeting social needs	*77*	*67*	*87*	*72*	*89*	*74*	*50*	*57*	*63*	*80*	***73***
Teaching courses	*74*	*63*	*60*	*56*	*28*	*71*	*20*	*20*	*31*	*28*	***54***
Neighbourhood visitation	*31*	*44*	*63*	*30*	*24*	*48*	*33*	*40*	*19*	*15*	***34***
Street evangelism	*18*	*40*	*3*	*36*	*0*	*68*	*0*	*77*	*0*	*32*	***33***
Local/national politics	*19*	*7*	*24*	*2*	*29*	*19*	*30*	*5*	*6*	*16*	***14***
Local/national media	*16*	*2*	*3*	*5*	*18*	*13*	*20*	*18*	*6*	*10*	***11***
Base (=100%)	1,031	365	381	328	427	270	79	1,450	144	496	**4,791**

More Roman Catholics and New Churches are involved in neighbourhood visitation than other denominations, and the URC and Smaller denominations less so. The New Churches and Pentecostals especially engage in street evangelism, while Anglicans, Roman Catholics, Methodists, the Orthodox and URC much less.

Methodists are particularly engaged in local or national politics and media, while the Independents and Orthodox do so less than others. However, "many of the Orthodox Communities (both 'Byzantine' and 'Oriental') are highly politicised – but in relation to politics in their home countries. As a result, they are active in approaching politicians and the media in respect of their own problems."[69]

By size of church

Likewise, these varied by size of church, as shown in Table A13 in the Appendix which indicates the larger churches are the most active in the majority of these community activities (though not in street evangelism), as might be expected. There is a particularly sizeable jump between the percentages for under 100, and 100 or more, in the holding of teaching courses and local/national media, suggesting crucial volunteers for both of these is not easily available in smaller churches.

Commitment of congregation

Question 21 asked two questions, the first in three parts. This first question asked about the commitment of members of the congregation to the Christian faith. Answers were:

- 70% were active members/regular attenders
- 22% were committed to the Christian faith but not active, and
- 8% were not yet personally committed to the Christian faith.

These percentages did not vary significantly by denomination, except for the Orthodox whose percentages were, respectively, 58%, 42% and 0%, and the last category for Smaller denominations where the percentage was 12%. Likewise, they did not vary by churchmanship or size of church, although the middle percentage was higher the larger the church (from 20% for churches with congregations of under 26 to 25% to churches with over 200); showing the larger the church, the increasing number of "passengers" it has.

The variation by Borough is shown in a Table in *Church Statistics*. There were six Boroughs where the percentage not yet personally committed to the Christian faith was greater than 10%: the City of Westminster (15%), Hackney (13%), Greenwich and Richmond upon Thames (12% each), and Harrow and Waltham Forest (11% each).

A report on the trends in the Anglican Diocese of London (broadly north and north-west of London) between 2003 and 2010 showed membership had "continued to grow strongly while attendance has begun to fall slightly", and it concluded committed people may be coming to church less often, something important to watch in subsequent years.[70] Such might be true for Anglicans in other Dioceses in London and for non-Anglican denominations.

In 2012, the Diocese of London launched "Capital Vision 2012" focussing on building "a church for London that is Confident, Compassionate and Creative", with special encouragement from the Bishop of London, the Rt Revd and Rt Hon Richard Chartres.[71]

Coming from another religion

Were those in the current congregation members of another religion when they first came? On average, 6% were. For the smallest congregations this was less so (3%) and more for the largest (8%), but the greatest variations were among those in the Smaller denominations (13%) and Pentecostals (11%). It did not vary by churchmanship.

Figure 6.11: Percentage of congregation coming from another religion, 2012

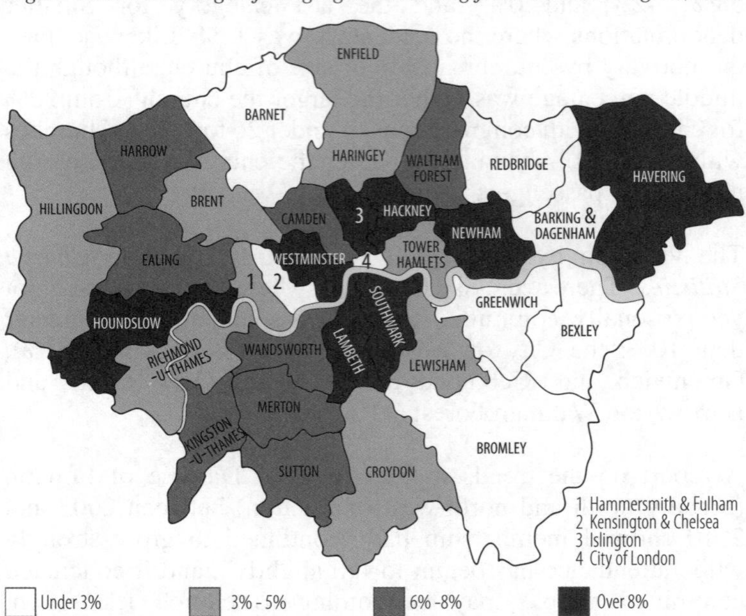

It varied somewhat by Borough, however, with the actual

percentages again given *Church Statistics*, and illustrated in Figure 6.11. The question did not ask for details of the other religions (and presumably atheism was not counted), but comparing the maps in Figures 2.7, and 6.11, would suggest the other religion was probably not Islam except perhaps in the City of Westminster and Newham.

So what does all this mean?

This Chapter has looked at the various church activities undertaken by congregations in London. A fifth, 21%, of churches used hired premises, markedly New Churches and Pentecostals. Three-fifths (63%) hold a mid-week service with an average of 55 people. This percentage and number is much greater than across England as a whole in 2005 (respectively 42% and 29 people). Those attending mid-week are five years older on average than Sunday churchgoers (which attracts more children). Churches of all sizes are active mid-week. About seven in every eight of these mid-weekers (86%) also attend church on a Sunday (not necessarily the same church). Mid-week worship is especially important for a significant number of Christians in Inner London.

Almost half, 45%, of London's churches have some kind of mid-week activity for young people; average attendance is about 30. While attendance was similar to the national level in 2005, again the percentage of churches holding such activities was greater (45% to 27%). Once more, Inner London has slightly more *pro rata* than Outer London. About three-quarters, 76%, were estimated to attend church on a Sunday.

In addition, about a quarter of London's churches, 23%, ran other kinds of mid-week activity especially for the local community, a percentage similar to the 2005 national percentage, but drawing an average of 71 people per week, rather higher than nationally (55).

This mid-week activity shows London's churches are generally more active than elsewhere, with Inner London on the whole slightly more active than Outer London. The consequence is a number of people attend mid-week but not on a Sunday, a number equivalent to an extra sixth, 16%, of Sunday attendance, bringing total church involvement to just over 10% of the capital's population.

Three-quarters, 73%, had a programme for meeting social needs – as Canadian Reg Bibby says, "People don't want churches, they want ministry!"[72] Half, 54%, held teaching courses of some kind. A third, 34%, were actively involved with neighbourhood visitation or street evangelism, and perhaps one in eight in local or national politics or media.

Over two-thirds, 70%, of congregations were deemed to be active, regular members, a fifth, 22%, committed but inactive, and 8% yet to make a personal commitment. About 6% of congregations initially came from another religion, especially in a few Boroughs – the City of Westminster, Hackney, Havering, Hounslow, Islington, Lambeth, Newham and Southwark.

7

Church Planting

The final section of the Census form was labelled "Church Origins" and asked questions about how the current congregation had started and developed. It focussed on church planting, and, after the first question, was only meant to be answered by those whose congregations had begun within the previous 20 years (that is, since 1992). Inevitably perhaps, a few respondents answered the questions although their churches had started more than 20 years previously, and some who should have completed this section either omitted it entirely or only answered some of the questions. This Chapter looks at all the given answers, without checking the accuracy of the 20-year period (in order to be able to use the maximum number of replies).

Church plants

"Has your church started or planted another church or another congregation since 1992? If so, how many?" was the first part of Question 22a. All respondents should have answered this question, but only 84% did so. Had they started another church it is likely they would have said so, so we have assumed those who did not answer the question did not start one. In an entirely separate survey also carried out in 2012 (for the Langham Partnership), but just of British evangelical ministers, a similar question found 19% of them had started another church in recent years.[73]

One church in seven, 15%, had started another church within the last 20 years or so, and of these half had started just one church, a quarter had started two, and the final quarter three or more. One minister said he had planted 18 churches, and another 15, but these were the exceptions. As the questionnaire was completed by ministers of churches in London it could be presumed that the churches started were also in the city, but this question was not actually asked. As the number of churches planted well exceeds the church increase in London since 1992, then either many of new churches were started outside the London area or were not successful.

It is difficult to judge how many new churches failed, but the Pentecostal experience in the north-west of England in the mid-1990s, focussing around the JIM [Jesus In Me] campaign, found that one plant in four failed within two years. That broad ratio seemed to be roughly replicated in the Langham survey, judging by the comments made by the ministers concerned. In overall terms, the number of newly started churches, grossed up for all churches in London, would amount to perhaps 1,700 new churches since 1992.[74] If a quarter of these failed,[75] then the actual number which were successful would be of the order of 1,300, about the number currently meeting which have actually started in London in the last 20 years.

The second part of Question 22 asked how many of the churches started were still meeting regularly, and 93% said they were, suggesting a much lower recent failure rate than others have experienced. Some 15% of churches who had planted a church said they were considering planting one or more future churches.

Which denominations are planting new congregations? The Pentecostals have started the most with a third, 32%. These are followed by the Anglicans (18%) and the Smaller denominations (15%); the groups which have spearheaded the growth in new London churches. Churches with an existing congregation of 100 or more are twice as likely to start another congregation as smaller churches.

How churches were started

Respondents were asked to indicate how their new congregations were started. Details are given in Table 7.1:

Table 7.1: How new congregations were initiated

Denomination	A %	B %	RC %	I %	M %	NC %	O %	P %	URC %	SD %	**Overall %**
Planted by individual or small group	*15*	*70*	*0*	*58*	*100*	*31*	*100*	*49*	*0*	*50*	***43***
Planned offshoot from a mother congregation	*60*	*15*	*33*	*14*	*0*	*31*	*0*	*29*	*0*	*19*	***30***
Initiative by a denomination or church-planting organisation	*20*	*15*	*67*	*14*	*0*	*15*	*0*	*20*	*100*	*12*	***19***
Other ways	*5*	*0*	*0*	*14*	*0*	*23*	*0*	*2*	*0*	*19*	***8***
% of total starts	*18%*	*12%*	*2%*	*6%*	*1%*	*12%*	*1%*	*32%*	*1%*	*15%*	**948**

A=Anglican. B=Baptist. RC=Roman Catholic. I=Independent. M=Methodist. NC=New Churches. O=Orthodox. P=Pentecostal. SD=Samller Denominations

Over two-fifths (43%) of new churches were started through an individual or a planning group. There were very few new Methodist or Orthodox churches; these had all been started this way. A third (30%) of new churches were planned offshoots from a mother congregation, something especially true of new Anglican churches. Holy Trinity Brompton and St Helen's, Bishopsgate are examples of this. About a fifth (19%) of the new churches were a specific denominational or organisational initiative, particularly some institutional denominations like the Roman Catholics or United Reformed. These figures did not vary significantly by other factors.

What were the other ways in which churches might start? Not many alternatives were described, but the majority were because of an existing church splitting, or because of two or more churches merging, largely when they were Local Ecumenical Partnerships [LEPs] which were consolidating. A few churches had started because of a desire to focus on a specific type of ministry, for example, among the homeless. One new church started, so the respondent wrote, because it was "ordered by the Queen"!

About one church in six, 18%, existed because it merged with another church, or formally joined another congregation. Some of these mergers (about a fifth) had happened early in the life of the church (within the first five years), but more had happened after a church had been meeting for five or 10 years. Others of these mergers were comparatively recent, suggesting perhaps the recession, or other external factors, may have necessitated the merger.

Some would assert church planting depends on what people think the church is. "The church does what it is. . . . If the church believes that the building is the primary place where God meets the needs of the people in the world then the leaders give importance for the church building and for the programmes that take place in the church."[76]

Influence on the new plant

More than half the churches (56%) said that a particular organisation, person or resource had been a major influence on the church plant. This was especially true for Baptists and New Churches, but far less true for new churches within the Smaller denominations. A long list of names was mentioned, and if this is a typical sample, then denominations, individual churches, organisations and specific people have all helped stimulate the planting of new churches in the last 20 years in London.

Denominations (21 were mentioned)

African Methodist Episcopal Zion Church; Baptist Union; Christ Apostolic Church; Church of God in Christ; Church of God of Prophecy; Flaming Headquarters (in Sierra Leone); Grace Baptist Partnership; Jesuits; Legion of Mary; the United Pentecostal Church and the United Reformed Church.

Organisations (19 were mentioned)

Churches in Community International; Co-Mission; Dolphin School; Equippers' Network International; Evangelical Alliance; Irish Episcopal Council for Immigrants; Jack Miller World Harvest Mission; Message of the Hour; MSC (France); Mustard-Seed Foundation Home Mission; Rhema Bible Training Centre (South Africa); Trans-Atlantic Alliance of Churches; Urban Expression and Vineyard.

Churches (17 were mentioned)

Holy Trinity, Brompton; Ichthus Christian Fellowship; Kensington Temple; Langley Chapel; Living Waters Foursquare Church; New Covenant Church, Brixton; Newfrontiers; Praise Chapel International; Salem Church; St Anne's, Limehouse; St Botolph's, Aldersgate; St Helen's, Bishopsgate; St Paul's, Shadwell and St Stephen's, Twickenham.

People (12 were mentioned)

Bishop Anthony; John and Carol Ascot (Toronto); Bishop Leon Edgar; Philip Edwards; Rev Dr P Jinadu; Martin Phelps; Jenny Sinnaovrai; Rick Warren and unnamed people like our Lay Reader, our Pastor, our Senior Pastor or white South African attenders.

Advertising was not listed as a possibility, but given the abundance of such opportunities in London, with many churches taking advantage of such, this also must be a factor, though unmeasured. Likewise word-of-mouth is crucial in starting any new enterprise, including new churches.

At the start of a new church

"When your church plant started, how many were present at its first Sunday service?" The average was 28 people, with New Churches, Anglicans and Baptists slightly more (average of 44, 39 and 32 respectively) and Pentecostals, Smaller denominations and Independents slightly less (average of 23, 20 and 17 respectively). There was no significant variation by churchmanship or area (Inner London 29; Outer London 27).

Churches with a present size of between 100 and 200 had slightly bigger start-ups than the largest churches of over 200 people (43 to 31), and both bigger than start-ups with smaller churches (21 if present congregation 50 or under).

Leadership

What kind of pastoral leadership was present at the church's start?

- 53% Full-time
- 20% Part-time
- 14% Lay-led
- 7% Bi-vocational
- 6% Missionary-led.

Anglicans, Independent churches, Pentecostals and Smaller denominations broadly followed this pattern, but the few churches started by the Methodists, Orthodox or Roman Catholics all had full-time leaders. New Churches also had a higher percentage of full-time leaders (71%), while Baptists had many more which were lay-led or missionary-led (54% between them).

Unsurprisingly, the larger the supporting church, the more likely the new plant was to have full-time leadership at the beginning.

Age of the minister

What was "the age then of the minister?" Younger than the current leaders of churches! Their average was 46 against the average age of an existing church leader of 54 (see Page 102). Table 7.2 gives the comparison.

Table 7.2: Age of leaders

Group	Under 30 %	30 to 39 %	40 to 49 %	50 to 59 %	60 to 69 %	70 or over %	Average age
Leader of a new church	*6*	*24*	*33*	*29*	*<–8–>*		46
Leader of existing church	*<–10–>*		*24*	*37*	*22*	*7*	54

The age did not vary significantly by denomination, but the few Methodist, Orthodox and URC leaders asked to help with a new church were closer to the average age of an existing church leader than other new plant leaders. There was no variation in age by churchmanship, size of present church, or location.

The Langham Partnership survey found those starting churches in their 40s or younger were slightly more likely to experience failure perhaps suggesting experienced leadership is essential for successful plants.[77]

Budget

The average budget was about £25,000 per new church, or roughly £1,000 per initial attender. There were a few Boroughs, all in Outer London, where this average was considerably exceeded, but it is impossible to know how truly representative these replies were. Anglicans and New Churches tended to have larger budgets (double the average) while Baptists, Pentecostals and Smaller denominations had to settle for much less.

Again, the churches which were currently between 100 and 200 in size were the most generous in helping with a plant's budget, and churches currently between 51 and 100 also provided about double the average budget for their newly started churches.

Target membership

Was the new church intended to reach a particular group of people? Yes, in half (48%) of cases, a percentage more true of Anglicans (88%), and less of Pentecostals (28%) and New Churches (23%). This did not vary by size of current church or Borough; however, Mainstream Evangelicals focussed on a particular group of people (74%), more than other churchmanships.

Who were the people these new churches sought to reach? They were in different groups:

Particular nationalities/language groups: Afro-Caribbeans, Black Africans, Coptic Egyptians, Czechs, Gujuratis, Irish immigrants, Portuguese, Romanians, Spanish and Hindi, Tamil and Urdu speakers, and so on.

Specific locational area/group: Canary Wharf workers, City workers, Docklands, Fulham community, Greenwich Borough, Isle of Dogs inhabitants, local Council Estate, local families, transient workers in Clapham, Wanstead inhabitants, workers in Moorgate, and so on.

Individual denominational members: Methodists, Roman Catholics and their neighbours, Southwark Quakers, etc.

Certain kinds of people: Senior citizens, the marginalised, people with faith who don't attend church, people seeking for a deeper link with God, students, the unchurched, the unreached, young professionals, youth, and so on.

When the new church was five years old

At the five-year point what was the average congregation? This question was only answered by 85% of those who answered the previous question. Does this mean 15% of these new churches failed in under 5 years? If so, that is a better average than was found by the Pentecostals in the 1990s, as previously explained. Perhaps more likely though is that the "parent" church had left the church plant to its independence and, therefore, may not have a record of the congregation after five years.

For those who answered both questions, the average congregation five years later had almost tripled, to an average of 76 people. It increased most for New Churches (average 103) and least for Baptists (average 33), but it did not increase significantly more than the average for the Pentecostal churches.

The increase was almost the same for Inner London and Outer London (77 and 75 respectively). However, where the supporting church was larger (that is, more than 100 in the congregation), their new plants did increase by a greater number (to an average of 140 people, twice the overall average), suggesting leadership guidance, financial resources and a greater pool of people to draw on for expertise were all crucial factors in a new church's viability.

Congregational change

How much did the initial congregation expand by during the first five years? By subtracting the original size from the five year size it is possible to estimate the range of change. One church in eight, 12%, saw their numbers decline, and a further 11% saw them remain static. Of the remaining 77%:

- 17% saw their numbers increase by up to 10 people
- 15% saw their numbers increase by between 11 and 20 people
- 14% saw their numbers increase by between 21 and 50 people, and
- 31% saw their numbers increase by over 50 people.

Given a starting average of 28 people, slightly under half (45%) saw their numbers double. However, the overall average number attending five years later was 76 people, because a small number of churches (11%) had seen incredibly rapid growth into triple figures.

Growing the church

How many of those attending after five years were previously active churchgoers? The average percentage was three-fifths (62%), suggesting 38% of the 76 attending, or 29 people, were not previously active, and therefore were "new".

If the figures in this Chapter are a reasonable sample of church planting experience across London, then it means of the 4,800 churches now in the city, some 1,100 new churches (currently in existence) have been planted in the last 7 years (some outside London and offsetting those which have closed), and that perhaps some 80,000 more people are attending church in London than before, rather more than a third of whom were previously non-churchgoers who have been added because of the church planting efforts of many existing churches. Does church planting work? YES! Is it worth all the hard work? YES!

The Langham Partnership survey asked if a suitable opportunity arose whether the leadership would seek to plant another church. In total, 97% said yes, they would.

Finance

The final question in this section asked whether, five years on, the new church was financially self-supporting. Only 5% of respondents didn't know; of the 95% who did, three-quarters (76%) said the plant was self-supporting now.

So what does all this mean?

The final section of the Census form focussed on questions about church planting. One church in seven, 15%, had started at least one further church in the previous 20 years (since 1992). While the number started which subsequently closed is unknown, of the order of 1,300 have been started, with at least 1,100 of these still in existence located within the Greater London area. They are part of the London church scene which this London Church Census has attempted to capture and describe.

Over two-fifths (43%) of these churches were started by an individual or small group, and a further third (30%) were planned as an offshoot of an existing congregation. A fifth (19%) were started as a result of a denominational or organisational initiative. The variation in the type of denomination, organisation, church congregation or person so involved is considerable.

Half (53%) of these new churches started with full-time leadership and a fifth (20%) with part-time. The average budget was £25,000, much of which one presumes was spent on the salary of the leader. These leaders were nearly 10 years younger than the average minister in London.

These new churches were sometimes targeted at particular nationalities, sometimes for certain groups of people, sometimes in a given location, and sometimes for those of the same denomination.

The average new church started with 28 people and, five years later, had grown to an average of 76 people, although this average is somewhat skewed because of the small number of churches which had grown greatly in this period. Rather than triple in attendance over a five-year period, the more normal experience was to double, and, of that increase, some would be existing churchgoers, perhaps three-fifths (62%) of the church five years later, while the other 38% were new people.

Grossed up, these numbers suggest that of the extra 80,000 people attending church in London from 20 years ago, just over a third do so because of the new churches. It also indicates the other two-thirds of the growth has come through the growth of existing churches, and also from those who were already churchgoers, perhaps in another country, before moving to London.

What of the theology?

This has been a statistical evaluation, but what of the theology of church planting in the city? Many have written on such, but we end with the conclusions of Benjamin Becker, Professor of Missiology, based in Lyon, who said the church-in-mission needs to:

- Comprehend that the essence of the city is not a random collection of sociological phenomena under purely secular powers, but rather a profoundly spiritual entity – the locus of spiritual powers vying for the souls of men.
- Rejoice in the knowledge that the Scriptures portray a merciful and loving Creator who progressively takes pains to accommodate man's insistence on city-building and city-dwelling, sovereignly carving out spaces in cities where His redemptive purposes may operate in the midst of human perversion and rebellion.
- Marvel at God's sovereign election of the human city – the very symbol of man's rejection of God – as the epicentre of His salvific act in Christ and His ongoing loving actions in human history, and understand God's election has resulted in the localisation of the conflict of the ages in the world's cities.

- Be liberated to be intentionally, pro-actively, and strategically present in the cities, to engage their inhabitants both intelligently and in the power of the Holy Spirit.[78]

The Challenges of the Census

The essential motivation of the 2012 London Church Census for the London City Mission (LCM) was to "look on the fields, white already to harvest". How could the LCM best deploy its workers in the days ahead, and where were the neediest unevangelised parts of London? The question is relevant to other cities, to denominations and organisations apart from the LCM, and for evangelism generally.

London is unique in England, at present, in that its churches are growing and people are flocking to them. Some 620,000 churchgoers in 2005 have become 720,000 in 2012, a 16% growth. Where there were 4,100 churches in 2005 there are now 4,800, a 17% growth. Such figures are impressive by any standard. What are the key features behind them?

1) Church Planting

Firstly, there is much growth in certain Inner London Boroughs where black people live. Inspired perhaps by the Redeemed Christian Church of God's desire to "plant a church within 10 minutes walking distance", many individuals or small groups of people are renting premises, sometimes from an existing church (a fifth of London's churches rent out their premises to another church), and starting worship services for their neighbours. A third (32%) of attenders lives within half a mile of their church. Two-fifths (43%) of London's new churches have started in this way. Three-fifths (57%) of those inaugurating them are in their 30s or 40s. What inspires them? A deep desire to reach their neighbours, perhaps motivated by the clear biblical teaching of some of the leaders of the very sizeable black churches – Jesus House, Ruach Ministries, Glory House or House of Praise. Added to this is key strategic leadership enthusing others to go and take a risk for the sake of the Kingdom, often in a specific location. Imagine the impact on London and the rest of the country if most of our churches were able to plant a new church!

2) Specialist Churches

Secondly, there is growth in churches offering a special outreach to particular groups of people, in this case often immigrants who welcome services in their own language. Many, but not all, of these are Evangelical, and not a few are Catholic (ministering especially to those from Roman Catholic countries). These are often located in Inner London where decent Sunday transport already exists. Not all of these are focussed on the needs of newcomers, as some, like Hillsong, offer a different type of worship. Others, more in Outer London, offer what is often called "Messy Church". The key here is starting an outreach focussed on particular groups of individuals, based on a social, ethnic, or age-related concern. For those who feel their present local church situation does not meet their needs, this type of ministry could revitalise areas where the church seems to be stagnating or irrelevant.

3) Growth in Larger Churches

Thirdly, many of the larger churches (of all ethnicities) are seeing substantial growth within their own congregations. This is especially true in Inner London, and especially so among those aged 20 to 44. A third (35%) of Inner London's attenders are in this age-group, almost double the 20% across England generally. What attracts these young or middle-aged people? Again many, but not all, of these churches are Evangelical, providing clear Bible-based expository teaching, often supported by Alpha or Christianity Explored teaching courses, which draw hundreds of those in their 20s. Some are Charismatic, like Holy Trinity Brompton, while others are Reformed, like St Helen's, Bishopsgate. With other research showing poor transmission of faith in Christian households, and often declining youth work in churches, many in their late teens or 20s lack basic clarity on how to live out their Christian life, and the essential doctrines behind their belief. These churches are providing that teaching, as in other larger churches across the country.

4) Unique Opportunities

Fourthly, London has an almost unique advantage and, therefore, challenge – it is where so many young people come for employment. The larger London churches are able to take advantage of a sociological phenomenon of, in many cases, relatively mobile people. Also, people of a similar sociological or educational background coming together regularly can be conducive for fellowship, friendship, and regular attendance (London worshippers come more frequently to church than those elsewhere). Here, again, is an opportunity for each church to assess the sociological, employment and educational mix (or unique features) in their area, and make their church and worship "user-friendly", for example, for students.

5) A Diverse Ethnicity

Fifthly, there is no doubt London is special because of its ethnic make-up. A third (31%) of its population is Asian or Black, compared with just 8% in the rest of England. That brings its own cultural challenge. There is also a religious divide – 12% of London's population is Muslim compared with 3% across the rest of England, and a further 10% are other religions, against 2% in the rest of England. Also, 6% of those in new churches were reckoned to come from other faiths, almost certainly a figure much higher than elsewhere. Other UK cities attract many from alternative ethnicities too. Is there a place for those of other cultures in our traditional London, and UK churches, as they are, or is one of the challenges of the London Census to transform a middle-class, white stereotype into a warm, all-embracing New Testament fellowship?

6) Key Age and Gender Focus

Sixthly, perhaps the principal challenge arising from the Census, is the need to attract back to our congregations the young marrieds or those living together, their teenagers and children, particularly the men of such families. At present, London's churches are attracting women far more than men. However, in reaching those with young-families (30s and 40s), churches are, in their own way, also providing for the next generation. Many churches in Outer London find they have fewer young people attending, having lost the vital "Sunday School years" to football and other sports, shopping, socialising, and so on. Recent Inner London experience suggests quality teaching is a key draw, together with imaginative provision for children.

7) Focussed Leadership

Lastly, only two-thirds (67%) of London churches have a paid ordained leader, while a fifth (22%) have a paid non-ordained leader. Half (49%) employ someone part-time. Many leaders, especially Pentecostal ministers, have a full- or part-time paid job and serve their church unpaid in their spare time. One church in eight has a full- or part-time youth worker, although this ratio is double in the Anglican and New Churches. Leaders stay slightly longer in their role in London than elsewhere. Far fewer look after more than one church (7% to 32% generally), so are able to focus more on a single congregation. Three-fifths (63%) of London's churches hold a mid-week service (against 42% elsewhere), and half (45%) a mid-week youth activity (against 27% elsewhere). Half (54%) run teaching courses, a third (34%) undertake neighbourhood visitation and street evangelism. One in seven leaders (15%) had started another church in recent years, delegating to a leader on average eight years younger (with half seeing numbers at least double within five years). Enabling leaders to have undivided responsibility for a single congregation (with clear targets) has almost certainly helped the incredible growth seen across London.

The focal challenges of the London Church Census involve location, leadership, culture, ethnicity, gender and age. Above all, these require clear thinking, impassioned praying, and strategic action. This study will have failed if it only results in academic agreement (or disagreement!). It will have succeeded only if churches are driven to prayer, and then to such actions as:

- Exploring the possibility of a church plant;
- Identifying key features of a locality for outreach;
- Considering an evangelism teaching course;
- Developing a Bible-based teaching ministry, perhaps mid-week;
- Freeing leadership solely for the task in hand (focussing on one church not several);
- Providing for a youth worker; and
- Expanding outreach among professionals, students, men, immigrants, the elderly, disabled, singles, those of alternative faiths and other specialist groups.

The fields *are* ready for harvest.

Appendix: Additional Tables

Table A1: Number of Churches in London, 1979-2020E

Year	1979	1989	1998	2005	2010	2012	2015E	2020E
Inner	1,424	1,594	1,821	1,981	2,207	2,383	2,442	2,560
Outer	1,926	1,965	2,041	2,106	2,373	2,408	2,425	2,470
Total	**3,350**	**3,559**	**3,862**	**4,087**	**4,580**	**4,791**	**4,867**	**5,030**

Table A2: Percentage of churchgoers in London by age-group, 1979-2020E

Age group	<11 %	11-14 %	15-19 %	20-29 %	30-44 %	45-64 %	65-74 %	75-84 %	85 & over %	Base (=100%)
1979[1,2]	*20*	*6*	*8*	*12*	*20*	*19*	*8*	*6*	*1*	687,700
1989[1]	*18*	*6*	*7*	*12*	*20*	*21*	*9*	*6*	*1*	649,600
1998[1]	*15*	*6*	*6*	*12*	*20*	*22*	*11*	*6*	*2*	617,900
2005[2]	*15*	*6*	*6*	*10*	*21*	*22*	*11*	*6*	*2*	623,000
2012	***14***	***7***	***5***	***11***	***21***	***21***	***12***	***7***	***2***	**721,500**
2020E	*13*	*7*	*4*	*11*	*21*	*21*	*13*	*8*	*2*	704,100

[1] Under 15 and 65 & over splits estimated pro rata to population [2] Revised figures E = Estimate

Table A3: Percentage of Male churchgoers in London, 2012

Males	Under 11 %	11-14 %	15-19 %	20-29 %	30-44 %	45-64 %	65-74 %	75-84 %	85 & over %	Average age	Base (=100%)
Inner	*14*	*7*	*5*	*14*	*21*	*21*	*10*	*6*	*2*	*39*	126,100
Outer	*17*	*7*	*7*	*9*	*19*	*21*	*12*	*6*	*2*	*39*	189,900
Total	*16*	*7*	*6*	*11*	*20*	*21*	*11*	*6*	*2*	*39*	316,000

Table A4: Percentage of Female churchgoers in London, 2012

Females	Under 11 %	11-14 %	15-19 %	20-29 %	30-44 %	45-64 %	65-74 %	75-84 %	85 & over %	Average age	Base (=100%)
Inner	*12*	*6*	*5*	*13*	*21*	*21*	*13*	*7*	*2*	41	168,900
Outer	*14*	*6*	*5*	*9*	*21*	*22*	*13*	*8*	*2*	42	236,600
Total	*13*	*6*	*5*	*11*	*21*	*22*	*13*	*7*	*2*	42	405,500

Table A5: Number of people attending church in London by age and gender, 2005 and 2012

Age group	2005		2012		Change per annum 2005-2012		
	Men	Women	Men	Women	Men	Women	Total
Under 11	50,639	46,019	49,249	53,566	-199	+1,078	+879
11 to 14	19,553	16,946	22,063	23,954	+359	+1,001	+1,360
15 to 19	22,263	12,460	19,188	18,669	-439	+887	+448
20 to 29	30,234	35,548	35,920	45,173	+812	+1,375	+2,187
30 to 44	64,711	68,477	63,780	85,130	-133	+2,379	+2,246
45 to 64	59,936	79,585	66,298	87,463	+909	+1,126	+2,035
65 to 74	31,150	37,380	35,672	52,527	+646	+2,164	+2,810
75 to 84	16,033	22,263	18,692	29,797	+380	+1,076	+1,456
85 & over	3,573	6,230	5,091	9,268	+217	+434	+651
Total	298,092	324,908	315,953	405,547	+2,552	+11,520	+14,072

Table A6: Age of congregation by denomination in numbers, Greater London, 2012

Age gp	Angl'n	Baptist	R Cath	Indep't	Method	New Ch	Ortho.	Pente	URC	Smaller	Total
Und 11	10,100	6,600	26,100	4,700	1,400	7,000	1,900	39,200	1,000	5,500	103,500
11-14	3,800	2,200	10,200	2,300	600	2,300	1,200	19,500	300	3,900	46,300
15-19	2,600	1,700	8,300	1,400	400	1,600	1,600	14,800	100	1,300	33,800
20-29	9,700	4,000	17,800	3,000	700	8,500	2,100	29,900	400	5,400	81,500
30-44	15,300	8,200	34,800	5,200	1,400	10,600	3,800	61,000	800	8,700	149,800
45-64	19,800	9,900	40,800	6,500	4,700	8,400	4,700	46,700	1,700	11,500	154,700
65-74	13,700	5,400	34,600	3,900	4,600	3,000	2,400	12,600	1,700	6,800	88,700
75-84	7,800	2,900	19,300	1,900	3,600	1,300	2,100	4,300	1,400	4,100	48,700
85 & over	2,000	1,000	6,400	600	900	500	100	1,000	600	1,400	14,500
Total	84,800	41,900	198,300	29,500	18,300	43,200	19,900	229,000	8,000	48,600	721,500

The denominational totals are as given in Table 3.3, and are expressed as percentages in Table 4.11.

Table A7: Age of congregation by churchmanship in numbers, Greater London, 2012

Age group	Anglo-Catholic	Broad	Cath-olic	Broad Evang.	Mainst. Evan.	Charis. Evan	Total Evan	Liberal	Low Church	All others	Total
Und 11	2,700	2,400	26,500	2,000	24,900	31,300	58,200	6,100	3,600	4,000	103,500
11-14	2,200	1,100	11,400	600	10,000	15,000	25,600	1,900	1,600	2,500	46,300
15-19	1,200	800	9,600	600	6,500	11,300	18,400	1,300	700	1,800	33,800
20-29	1,900	2,600	18,500	1,100	24,400	24,700	50,200	2,900	2,000	3,400	81,500
30-44	3,800	4,800	38,900	2,700	34,200	48,200	85,100	6,100	4,400	6,700	149,800
45-64	3,400	5,200	39,700	3,800	36,200	42,200	82,200	9,300	6,500	8,400	154,700
65-74	4,600	3,700	30,300	2,500	20,000	11,900	34,400	6,700	5,000	4,000	88,700
75-84	2,300	2,200	15,800	1,600	11,200	4,900	17,700	4,200	3,300	3,200	48,700
85 & over	600	600	5,200	600	3,400	1,500	5,500	1,100	1,000	500	14,500
Total	22,700	23,400	195,900	15,500	170,800	191,000	377,300	39,600	28,100	34,500	721,500

The churchmanship totals are as given in Table 3.7, and are expressed as percentages in Table 4.13.

Table A8: Age of church ministers serving in London, by denomination, 2012

Age group	Angl'n %	Baptist %	R Cath %	Indep't %	Method %	New Ch %	Ortho. %	Pente %	URC %	Smaller %	Overall %
Under 30	*1*	*1*	*0*	*0*	*5* (Under 30 and 30-39 combined)	*0*	*0*	*0*	*0*	*2*	*1*
30-39	*7*	*15*	*5*	*10*		*16*	*5*	*4*	*7*	*16*	*9*
40-49	*24*	*29*	*16*	*27*	*9*	*25*	*10*	*29*	*7*	*26*	*24*
50-59	*44*	*29*	*40*	*25*	*45*	*40*	*17*	*40*	*40*	*31*	*37*
60-69	*22*	*18*	*26*	*21*	*36*	*16*	*45*	*16*	*40*	*22*	*22*
70 & over	*2*	*8*	*13*	*17*	*5*	*3*	*23*	*11*	*6*	*3*	*7*
Average age	54	52	58	56	57	52	62	55	58	51	54

Table A9: Percentage of London churchgoers by ethnicity, by denomination, 2012

Ethnicity	Angl'n %	Baptist %	R Cath %	Indep't %	Method %	New Ch %	Ortho. %	Pente %	URC %	Smaller %	Overall %
White	79	64	55	78	59	73	96	23	88	76	**53**
Mixed	3	4	3	5	2	4	1	9	3	1	**5**
Black	12	24	16	8	30	16	2	58	6	9	**28**
Asian	5	6	23	8	7	5	1	9	2	12	**12**
Other	1	2	3	1	2	2	0	1	1	2	**2**
Asian: I/P/B	2	2	13	3	2	2	0	6	0	4	**6**
Asian: C/J/K	2	2	3	2	3	2	1	1	2	7	**3**
Asian: Other	1	2	7	3	2	1	0	2	0	1	**3**
Base (=100%)	84,800	41,900	198,300	29,500	18,300	43,200	19,900	229,000	8,000	48,600	**721,500**

I/P/B=Indian/Pakistani/Bangladeshi. C/J/K=Chinese?Japanese?Korean

Table A10: Percentage of London churchgoers by ethnicity, by size of church, 2012

Size	White %	Mixed %	Black %	Asian %	Other %	Asian: I/P/B %	Asian: C/J/K %	Asian: Other %	Base (=100%)
Under 26	59	3	33	4	1	2	1	1	10,600
26 to 50	55	5	34	5	1	2	1½	1½	43,300
51 to 100	54	4	31	10	1	4	4½	1½	101,500
101 to 200	61	5	27	5	2	3	1	1	146,200
Over 200	50	5	28	15	2	8	2	5	419,900
Overall	53	5	28	12	2	6	3	3	721,500

I/P/B=Indian/Pakinstani/Bangladeshi. C/J/K=Chinese?Japanese?Korean

Table A11: Percentage of London churchgoers by ethnicity, by churchmanship, 2012

Ethnicity	Anglo-Catholic %	Broad %	Catholic %	Broad Evan. %	Mainst. Evan. %	Char'ic Evan. %	Total Evan. %	Liberal %	Low Church %	Other %	**Over-all %**
White	53	74	52	66	66	38	51	70	64	43	**53**
Mixed	4	4	4	4	4	5	5	6	4	12	**5**
Black	35	17	19	25	23	48	36	19	23	16	**28**
Asian	7	5	21	4	6	8	7	4	8	29	**12**
Other	1	0	4	1	1	1	1	1	1	0	**2**
Asian: I/P/B	2	2	11	3	2½	5	4	1½	2	0	**6**
Asian: C/J/K	2	2	3	½	2½	1	1½	½	4	29	**3**
Asian: Other	3	1	7	½	1	2	1½	2	2	0	**3**
Base (=100%)	22,700	23,400	195,900	15,500	170,800	191,000	377,300	39,600	28,100	34,500	**721,500**

I/P/B=Indian/Pakinstani/Bangladeshi. C/J/K=Chinese?Japanese?Korean. Mainst=Mainstream. Char'ic=Charismatic

Table A12: Percentage of London churchgoers by length of attendance at current church, by denomination, 2012

Length of attendance	Angl'n %	Baptist %	R Cath %	Indep't %	Method %	New Ch %	Ortho. %	Pente %	URC %	Smaller %	**Overall %**
< 3 yrs	24	23	19	21	14	34	13	26	15	25	**23**
3 - 5 yrs	19	18	15	15	15	21	70	27	11	15	**19**
6 - 10 yrs	20	22	23	20	18	24	2	24	11	19	**21**
11 - 20 yrs	17	19	20	23	21	12	4	14	20	18	**18**
> 20 yrs	20	18	23	21	32	9	11	9	43	23	**19**
Base (=100%)	84,800	41,900	198,300	29,500	18,300	43,200	19,900	229,000	8,000	48,600	**721,500**
Average time	10	10	12	11	14	7	7	8	16	11	**10 years**

Table A13: Community engagement by size of church of London churches, 2012

Size of church	25 or under %	26 to 50 %	51 to 100 %	101 to 200 %	Over 200 %	**Overall %**
Meeting social needs	*60*	*68*	*73*	*77*	*84*	***73***
Hold teaching courses	*29*	*40*	*57*	*65*	*69*	***54***
Neighbourhood visitation	*35*	*26*	*29*	*34*	*47*	***34***
Street evangelism	*25*	*27*	*35*	*38*	*32*	***33***
Local/national politics	*10*	*12*	*11*	*9*	*23*	***14***
Local/national media	*12*	*9*	*6*	*14*	*19*	***11***
Base (=100%)	590	870	1,221	990	1,120	**4,791**

Notes

1. Based on an interview with Boris Johnson by Chris Blackhurst reported in *Management Today*, January 2011, Page 30; religious data from *Religious Trends* No 6, 2006/2007, edited P W Brierley, Christian Research, Eltham, London, 2006 or the London Church Census 2012.
2. *Rome in the Ancient World*, David Potter, Thames and Hudson, London, 2009, Page 187.
3. Taken from *A Short History of London*, www.localhistories.org, accessed July 2013.
4. Especially tuberculosis and smallpox, as recorded in a Table of causes of death for 17th century Londoners, given in *The Daily Telegraph*, 5 December, 2011, as part of an exhibition at the Royal Society.
5. *The Shard: Official Guide Book*, Thames & Hudson, London, 2013, Page 7.
6. *I Never Knew That About London*, Christopher Winn, Ebury Press, Random House Group, 2011, various pages.
7. Article in *The Economist*, 30 June 2012.
8. *Localism in London*, Anna Turley and Joanna Wilson, Future of London, Portland Communications, March 2012.
9. *Decentralised Energy: Could London emulate Copenhagen?* London 2062, Future of London, UCL, 2012.
10. Article in *The Economist*, Special Report, 30 June 2012, Page 4.
11. Seminar "London 2062" at UCL, London, 19 September 2012, Ben Harrison, Director of Future of London.
12. Article in *The Economist*, 16 February 2013, Page 25.
13. The response to the mailed questionnaires was 14%, London Diocese a further 9%, with the remaining 31% extrapolated from earlier information. The direct response is lower than originally expected mostly because it would seem a high proportion of the letters with the Census forms were not delivered by Royal Mail (judging by the large number of requests subsequently received for a copy of the form). Even so, this rate of direct response is similar to many other professional studies.

14. *Being Built Together*, University of Roehampton, Churches Together in South London, Southwark for Jesus, Final Report, June 2013. The purpose of the project was to discover more information about Black Majority Churches in the Borough.
15. While the total is firm, the numbers for the denominations are all estimated.
16. Partly based on the experience of Assemblies of God churches in the north-west in the 1990s when, with the JIM [Jesus In Me] campaign they found one newly planted church in four closed within two years of opening.
17. A subsequent detailed private analysis of new and closed churches across each London postcode confirmed that the number of new churches started in the longer period 1998-2012 was about 1,200.
18. Figure 5.2 suggests 373 churches may be started between 2010 and 2019, which, should this figure be correct, will mean that 136 churches will close if the overall total of 5,030 in 2020 is to be maintained.
19. It is often thought that immigrants have poor educational qualifications. A 2008 study by the London School of Economics "showed that among migrants who had arrived in the previous 3 years, 61% had graduate-level qualifications, against 30% of native Londoners, and only 7% had no qualifications at all, against 24% of natives." (Article in *The Economist*, 30 June 2012, Special Report on London, Page 8).
20. ONS Census releases on their website, 11 December 2012 for 2011 figures. 2001 figures from *Religious Trends*, No 4, Christian Research, Eltham, London, 2002.
21. *Sleepwalking to segregation? Challenging myths about race and migration*, Nissa Finney and Ludi Simpson, Policy Press, Univ of Bristol, 2009.
22. Details are given on Page 2.7 of *UK Church Statistics 2005-2015*, ADBC Publishers, Tonbridge, 2011.
23. "Faith that won't fit the mould" by Linda Woodhead in *The Tablet*, 15 December 2012.
24. Op cit., Item 21.
25. *Travel in London* Report 3, Transport for London, 2010, Page 38.
26. ONS Census releases on their website, January 2013, Table KS404EW Car or Van availability.
27. *Religious Worship in England and Wales*, Census of Great Britain 1851, Horace Mann, George Routledge & Co., London, 1854.
28. *The Tide is Running Out*, Peter Brierley, Christian Research, Eltham, London, 2000, Page 227.
29. *The Religious Life of London*, Richard Mudie-Smith, Hodder & Stoughton, London, 1904.

30. Office of National Statistics website, Past trends in life expectancy.
31. The actual figures are for 2005, 2010 and 2012 respectively – London 623,000, 677,200 and 721,500. Rest of England 2,613,100, 2,405,800 and 2,321,500. Total 3,236,100, 3,083,000 and 3,043,000.
32. Such as that given in a report for Premier Radio in 2001 by Christian Research, which suggested the total attendance in 2016 might be only 542,000.
33. See article "C of E forecast to shrink" in *FutureFirst*, Brierley Consultancy, October 2012, Page 5.
34. See for example the writings of Dr Babatunde Adedibu, such as his paper "Faith without Borders: Maximising the Missionary potential of Britain's Black-Majority Churches", available from the Missional Network on the web, or his book *Coat of Many Colours*, The Origin, Growth, Distinctiveness and Contributions of Black Majority Churches to British Christianity, published by Wisdom Summit, Thamesmead, London in 2012.
35. Report in the *Church Times*, 19 October 2012, Page 8.
36. *Another Capital Idea*, Report for the Diocese of London, by Bob Jackson and Alan Piggot.
37. Annual Mission Returns by the Parish of St James with St Matthew at Muswell Hill.
38. *Religious Trends* No 6, 2006/2007, edited Peter Brierley, Christian Research, Eltham, London, 2006, Table 12.2.4.
39. These terms come from ministers ticking the relevant boxes on the Census form. Thus those ticking "Broad" and "Evangelical" are described as "Broad Evangelical" even if they ticked a third box, and those ticking "Charismatic" and"Evangelical" likewise are described as "Charismatic Evangelical". They would also be described as "Charismatic Evangelical" if they just ticked "Charismatic" unless they also ticked "Catholic". Those ticking just "Evangelical" – which many did – are described here as "Mainstream Evangelical" to distinguish them from the other two groups. This group has nothing ostensibly to do with the Mainstream Anglicans and Mainstream Baptists groups using the same term, although many Anglican or Baptist describing their churches as "Evangelical" are likely to be members of them.
40. So Wikipedia on Anglo-Catholicism, accessed July 2013.
41. See their website, accessed 23 February 2013.
42. BBC News, 5th London 2012, on their website, accessed 23rd February 2013.

43. It is not clear whether Kingston upon Thames should be spelt this way or as Kingston-upon-Thames. Similar concerns arise for Richmond upon Thames. That they used to have hyphens is certain; but neither of their official website now use them, so therefore they are not used here.
44. For those interested, a t-test was undertaken on the numbers counted and estimated by age group. The square root of the sum of squares was $s = 2{,}615$, $t = 1.32$, ν (degrees of freedom) = 14, $P = 0.107$, well within normal significance levels.
45. This suggestion is not true of Roman Catholic choirs.
46. Article in *The Economist*, 19 November, 2011, Page 32.
47. *Mirror* Report of Health Survey in 2010 found 27% of girls had lost their virginity by the age of 15 as had 22% of boys.
48. *Attitudes to Morality and Religion among Secondary-School-age young people*, Josh McDowell Report, Christian Research, Eltham, London, 2005.
49. From *Reaching and Keeping Tweenagers*, Peter Brierley, Christian Research, London, 2002, Pages 10-13.
50. Figures taken from ONS Census releases, op cit. Item 26, Table QS802EW.
51. Respectively for Under 11, 11 to 14, and 15 to 19 age-groups, the percentages are: Inner London 15%, 31%, 38%; Outer London 20%, 38%, 42%; Males 18%, 35%, 40%; Females 17%, 32%, 37%; against overall percentages of 17%, 33%, and 39%.
52. Taken from Table 2.3 of *Religious Trends* No 2, 2000/2001, Christian Research, Eltham, London, 1999.
53. *Pulling out of the Nosedive, What the 2005 English Church Census reveals*, Peter Brierley, Christian Research, Eltham, London, 2006, Page 180.
54. Op cit., Item 28, *Tide*, Page 168.
55. The 1998 figures come from *Church Growth in the 1990s*, a report for Springboard by Christian Research in 2000, and the figures for 2005 come from op cit., Item 53, *Nosedive*, Table 8.3.
56. The percentage is a total of the 21% in Figure 3.2 and the 4% in Table 3.3; the assertion about both larger churches and Independents coming from a report *The Significance of Larger Churches*, Brierley Consultancy, 2009.
57. Op cit., Item 22, *Church Statistics*, Table 1.1.1.
58. Op cit., Item 53, *Nosedive*, Page 145.
59. Growth by Fellowship & Evangelism at All Souls Church, Langham Place, Attendance Survey, Peter Brierley, Nov 1981.
60. Article in *The Economist*, 15 December, 2012, Page 25.
61. Op cit., Item 53, *Nosedive*, Page 214.

62. If one assumed that responding churches were a true sample of all churches then the total mid-week attendance would be 183,200, but it is known that an above average number of churches offering mid-week services only responded, so this number has been reduced by 10% for the analysis to 164,900
63. Report in *The Church of England Newspaper*, 7 April, 2013, Page 1.
64. Op cit., Item 22, *Church Statistics*, Page 2.3.
65. Article in *The Economist*, 22 September, 2012, Page 31.
66. The percentages were 87% in Inner London and 85% in Outer London.
67. Op cit., Item 53, *Nosedive*, Page 217.
68. Details may be obtained from Alex King, 51, Hugon Road, Fulham, London SW6 3ER.
69. Extracted comment from letter of 17th May 2013 from the Most Revd Gregorios Theocharous, Archbishop of the Greek Orthodox Archdiocese of Thyateira and Great Britain.
70. Op cit., Item 36, *Another Capital Idea*.
71. Details supplied by the Diocese of London; more information available from Andy Brookes, General Secretary and CEO at andy.brookes@london.anglican.org.
72. *A New Day: The Resilience and Restructuring of Religion in Canada*, Professor Reginald W Bibby, Project Canada Books, 2012, Page 26.
73. *Living the Christian Life*, Report for the UK & Ireland Langham Partnership, Part 2: Ministers, Brierley Consultancy, 2012, Chapter 6.
74. A number broadly supported by a detailed but approximate analysis given on Page 12.15 of *UK Church Statistics, 2010-2020*, which suggested that 1,919 churches had been started in London between 1989 and 2012.
75. The same analysis also suggested that the number of closures worked out as just under a quarter of new Inner London churches closed in this period (1989 to 2012) but perhaps half of new Outer London churches, although the closing churches would in most cases be existing churches rather than new church plants. The Outer London proportion is very uncertain.
76. Editorial "Church-Mission Dynamics" in *India Church Growth Quarterly*, Vol 19, No 3, Oct-Dec 2012, Page 2.
77. Op cit., Item 73, *Living*, Chapter 6.
78. Taken from *Vista*, the quarterly bulletin of research-based information on mission in Europe, Redcliffe College, Gloucester, Issue 11, October 2012, Page 2.

ABOUT BRIERLEY CONSULTANCY

Brierley Consultancy began in 2007, after its founder moved on from being the Executive Director of Christian Research for 14 years and European Director of MARC Europe for the 10 years prior to that. He has been the Senior Lausanne Associate for Church Research since 1994, and Associate since 1984. In 1972 he began what became in 1983 the *UK Christian Handbook* and when with Christian Research compiled 7 editions of *Religious Trends*. Brierley Consultancy is committed to:

Building vision for the future for individual churches and Christian agencies.

Interpreting the results from research and suggesting actions so that the Kingdom of God may grow.

Enabling strategic thinking in churches or agencies using the latest analyses of Christian life in the UK and the rest of the world.

A six-page bi-monthly bulletin called *FutureFirst* is published by Brierley Consultancy "providing facts for forward planning", a digest of contemporary statistical information on church and religious life. For a sample copy please write to the address below. It has received many plaudits from church and agency subscribers for its succinct but relevant articles.

The Consultancy happily works with all Trinitarian churches and organisations – Anglican, Methodist, Baptist, Presbyterian, Reformed, Independent, Catholic, Pentecostal, Charismatic, Orthodox and many smaller denominations. It does not work with non-Trinitarian groups such as the Jehovah's Witnesses or Mormons.

Peter Brierley is known in the UK for organising and analysing large scale Church Censuses of church attendance held in the various countries of the United Kingdom, the most recent of which, prior to the 2012 London Church Census, was the 2005 English Church Census, the results of which were published in September 2006.

Recent key publications include:

God's Questions, Vision, Strategy and Growth, ADBC Publishers, September 2010

Major UK Religious Trends 2010 to 2020, Brierley Consultancy, February 2011

21 Concerns for 21st Century Christians, ADBC Publishers, February 2011

Mission Workers in the 21st Century, ADBC Publishers, March 2011

UK Church Statistics 2005-2015, ADBC Publishers, June 2011

Living the Christian Life: Becoming like Jesus, ADBC Publishers, September 2012

London Churches are Growing!, Summary booklet, ADBC Publishers, June 2013

One-day seminars *Going for Growth* based on the book *God's Questions* were held in the autumn of 2011, and Conferences especially for leaders of larger churches are organised each year, the latter in association with CPAS. Peter is also a Trustee of several Christian charities.

Brierley Consultancy is headed by Dr Peter Brierley, a statistician with over 40 years of experience in working on Christian evaluation, research and publishing. For more information, contact him at:

The Old Post Office, 1 Thorpe Avenue,
Tonbridge, Kent TN10 4PW,
or by email: peter@brierleyres.com,
or phone +44 (0) 1732 369 303.
Website: www.brierleyconsultancy.com

Index

1851 Church Census 45, 51
1886 Survey 47
1903 London Census 48
2011 Population Census 35

Acholi (Ugandan) 30
Africaaners 29
African Methodist Episcopal Zion Church 136
African population 25, 26
Afro-Caribbeans 139
Age challenge 147
Age of:
- Churchgoers 77, 78, 152, 153
- Leaders 102
- Mid-week attenders 117
- New minister 138, 153

Agnostic population 37
Airspace 10
Aladura 29
Albanian 29
Alfred the Great 10
All Souls, Langham Place 75, 92, 103
All Saints', Plumstead 98
Allen, Beth 14
Alperton 31
Alpha courses 126, 146
American 29
Anglican:
- Age of attenders 95, 152
- Age of ministers 153
- Attendance 49, 56, 57, 119
- Christmas 104, 113
- Churches 23, 28, 47, 62, 75, 88, 89, 124
- Community activity 127, 128
- Deaths 38
- Distance from church 111
- Ethnicity 106, 107, 154
- Groups 16
- Leadership 99
- Length of attendance 109, 155
- Membership 38
- Mid-week 6, 115,118
- New church attendance 137
- Planting 7, 24, 134, 139
- Translated services 30
- Youth activities 121
- Youth workers 100

Anglo-Catholic:
- Age of attenders 89, 90
- Attendance 64, 65, 153
- Churches 5, 32
- Community activity 126
- Distance from church 111
- Ethnicity 108, 155
- Length of attendance 109

Antiochian 29
Apprentices, number 10
Arabic 30, 31
Armenian 29
Ascot, John and Carol (Toronto) 137
Ashimolowo, Matthew 69
Asian:
- Churchgoers 105, 106, 107, 154, 155
- Population 4, 25, 26, 147

Assemblies of God 17, 60
Assyrian 29, 30
Atheists 37, 40
Average age 78, 82, 95, 102
Average attendance 122

Baha'i population 36
Bangladeshi population 25, 26
Bank of England 11
Bankers 10
Baptist:
- Age of attenders 152
- Age of ministers 102, 153

Baptist (contd):
Attendance 49, 57
Churches 23, 24, 47, 63, 88, 89, 124
Community activity 127, 128
Deaths 39
Distance from church 111
Ethnicity 106, 107, 154
Length of attendance 109, 155
Mid-week 115, 118
New church attendance 137, 140
Translated services 30
Union 16, 136
Youth activities 121
Barking & Dagenham 27, 33, 67, 70, 72, 91
Barnet 21, 43, 51, 67, 91
Battersea, Nine Elms, 12
Becker, Prof Benjamin 143
Being Built Together 22
Bexley 25, 42, 51, 67, 70, 91, 92
Bibby, Reg 132
Bible belt 51
Bible Classes 102, 115
Big Ben 11
Billy Graham Crusade 11
Bishop Anthony 137
Black:
Africans 139
Attendance 4, 104, 105, 114, 154, 155
Churches growing 3
Majority Churches 22, 55, 60, 65, 74, 76
Population 4, 25, 147
Size of church 107
Black Death, The 11
Blackfriars 11
BMC *see* Black Majority Churches
Borough Growth 20
Boudicca revolt 10
Boyle, Danny 13
Boys under 15 80
Brazilian 29, 31
Brent 25, 33, 42, 43, 51, 67, 70, 72, 75, 76, 91
British Empire 11
British Weekly 47
Broad churchgoers:
Age of churchgoers 89, 90
Age of ministers 153
Attendance 5, 64, 65
Churches 32
Community activity 126
Distance from church 111
Ethnicity 108
Length of attendance 109, 155
Broad Evangelical:
Age of churchgoers 89, 90
Age of ministers 153
Attendance 64, 65
Churches 32
Community activity 126
Distance from church 111
Ethnicity 108
Length of attendance 109, 155
Bromley 42, 51, 67, 92
Brownell, Rev Dr Kenneth 14
Buddhist population 36, 37, 41, 42, 43, 50
Budget for new church 7, 139
Burmese 31
Bus passengers 44
Byelorussian 29

Caesar, Julius 10
Camden 5, 25, 42, 43, 51, 66, 69, 91
Canary Wharf workers 139
Canonbury 31
Cantonese (Chinese) 30
Capital Vision 2012 130
Car drivers 44
Car passengers 44
Caribbean population 25, 27
Cathedral choirs 80
Catholic:
Age of churchgoers 89, 90
Age of ministers 153
Attendance 64, 65, 76
Churches 32
Churchmanship 5
Community activity 126
Distance from church 111
Ethnicity 108
Length of attendance 109, 155
– *see also* Roman Catholic
Census of Population 35

Chapels, private 24
Chaplaincies, Roman Catholic 29
Charismatic Evangelical:
  Age of churchgoers 89, 90
  Age of ministers 153
  Attendance 64, 65
  Churches 32
  Community activity 126
  Distance from church 111
  Ethnicity 108
  Length of attendance 109, 155
Chartres, Rt Revd & Rt Hon Richard 130
Cherubim & Seraphim 29
Chessun, Rt Revd Christopher 98
Child attendance 49, 85
Children in families 82
Chinese 4, 25, 28, 29, 30, 31, 105, 108, 114
Christ Apostolic Church 136
Christadelphians 50
Christian Brethren 16, 58
Christian, meaning of 39
Christian population 36, 37, 41, 42, 43
Christianity Explored 126, 146
Christmas attendance 6, 104, 113
Church:
  Activities 115
  Attendance 53
  Number 151
  Planting 7, 133, 145
Church of England 28, 37, 39, 48
Church of God in Christ 136
Church of God of Prophecy 17, 136
Church of Pentecost 17
Churches in Community International 136
Churchgoers, number of 151
Churchmanship of churches 31
Churchmanship of churchgoers 64
City of London 5, 11, 21, 28, 31, 43, 47, 66, 69, 91, 92, 119
City of Westminster – *see* Westminster
City workers 139
Claudius, Emperor 10
Clifford, Steve 14
Closures 24, 141, 142
Co-habitation 82, 83
Co-Mission 136
Coles, Revd Canon John 14
Commitment of congregation 129
Community engagement 156
Companies, largest 9
Congolese 29, 31
Congregational churches 58
Congregational Federation 16
Constantine, Emperor 10
Coptic 29, 30
Coptic Egyptians 139
Cornwall 58
Cottrell, Rt Revd Stephen 14
Cradle Christians 39
Crematoria funerals 37
Croatians 29
Croydon 25, 67, 70, 72, 91, 92
Cultural challenge 147
Cyclists 44
Czechs 29, 139

Dagenham – *see* Barking and Dagenham
Daily News 48
Date church built 99
Deaf churches 30
Deaths 38, 39
Delaney, Ven Peter 116
Denominational initiatives 135
Diamond Jubilee 12
Digital capital 9
Diocese of London 13, 63, 65, 116, 129, 130
Distance lived from church 6, 110, 114
Docklands 139
Dolphin School 136
Dominion Theatre 75
Drinking by young people 80
Drop-in Centres 122
Druid population 36
Drummond, Capt Terry 14
Dunnett, Rev John 14
Dutch 29

Ealing 31, 43, 51, 67, 80, 91
Easter services 59
Edgar, Bishop Leon 137
Edgware 31
Edwards, Philip 137
El Shaddai 29
Elim Pentecostal 17, 60

Elizabeth II 12
Eltham College 1
Emmaus courses 126
Employment of leaders 100
Employment, seeking 147
Energy planning 12
Enfield 21, 25, 33, 51, 67, 70, 72, 76
Enfield Evangelical Free Church 58
England, population 36
Equippers' Network International 136
Eritreans 29, 31
Essex, Kingdom of 10
Estonian 29
Ethiopians 29, 31
Ethnicity 25, 39, 105, 147, 154
Euclid 1
Evangelical:
Age of churchgoers 89, 90
Age of ministers 153
Attendance 64, 65, 76
Churches 32, 58
Community activity 126
Distance from church 111
Ethnicity 108
Growth 65
Length of attendance 109, 110, 155
Presence 5
Specialist churches 146
Evangelical Alliance 136
Evangelical Fellowship of Congregational Churches 16
Evangelical Presbyterian Church 17
Eye, the 11

Faithful Christians 39
Families and children 82
Fanti (Ghana) 30
Fellowship of Churches of Christ 16
Female churchgoers 49, 80, 81, 117, 151, 152
FIEC 16, 58
Filipino population 26, 30
Financial centre 9
Fincham, Lt Col Melvin 14
Finnish 29
Finsbury Borough 47
Flaming Headquarters 136
Forecast 39
Fortnightly attendance 103
Free Church of England 16
Free Church of Scotland 17
Free Thinker population 37
French 29, 30
Frequency of attendance 102, 103
Fulham community 139
Full-time leaders 100, 138
Funerals 37
Fyffe, Revd Canon Bob 14

Gain in numbers 83, 84
Gaukroger, Revd Stephen 14
GDP highest 10
Gen X and Y 82, 83
Gender:
Churchgoers 77, 152
Leaders 102
German 29, 30
Gerry, James 116
Ghana 28, 29, 30
Gherkin, The 11
Glory House 145
Goan churches 28, 29, 114
God, belief in 40
Gospel Standard Baptist 16
Grace Baptist 16, 136
Gray, Rt Revd Graham 14
Great Exhibition 11
Great Fire 11
Greek 29, 30
Greek Orthodox Church 16
Greenwich 25, 33, 47, 67, 70, 91, 92, 129, 139
Growth of church 33, 141
Gujuratis 29, 30, 31, 139

Hackney 21, 25, 42, 43, 51, 66, 129, 132
Hammersmith & Fulham 21, 42, 66, 72
Hanwell 31
Harding, Mark 14
Haringey 25, 33, 64, 66, 69, 91
Harrow 31, 42, 43, 51, 67, 70, 76, 91, 95, 129
Havering 21, 42, 51, 67, 70, 132
Heavy Metal population 37
Higgins, George 1
Hillingdon 27, 43, 67, 91

Hillsong 58, 75, 80, 92
Hindu population 30, 36,37, 41, 42, 139
Holy Trinity, Brompton 75, 80, 92, 135, 137, 146
Hospital services 17
Hounslow 21, 27, 31, 42, 43, 51, 67, 91, 92, 132
House of Praise 75, 145
House Churches – *see* New Churches
Houses of Parliament 11
Housing planning 12
Humanist population 37
Hungarian 29, 30

Icelandic29
Ichthus Christian Fellowship 16, 137
Immigrant:
- Age of 85
- Churches 24, 55, 61
- Growth 3, 25
- Religion 35

Independent Baptists 16
Independent churches:
- Age of attenders 152
- Age of ministers 153
- Attendance 49, 57, 58
- Churches 23, 24, 47, 88, 89, 124
- Community activity 127, 128
- Distance from church 111
- Ethnicity 106, 107, 154
- Group 16
- Leadership 99
- Length of attendance 109, 155
- Mid-week 115, 118
- New church attendance 137
- Ownership of building 124
- Translated services 30
- Youth activities 120, 121

Indian population 25, 26, 29, 105
Individuals planting a church 135
Industrial Revolution 11, 46
Inner London 3, 19, 42, 49, 66, 68, 69, 72, 79, 81, 94, 108, 114, 115, 120, 131, 140, 146, 148
Iranian 29
Irish 29
Irish Episcopal Council for Immigrants 136, 139
Irukwu, Pastor Agu 14
Islam 130
Isle of Dogs inhabitants 139
Islington 5, 13, 21, 42, 43, 51, 66, 72, 91, 92, 95

Jack Miller World Harvest Mission 136
Jains population 36
Jamaat, Tablighi 70
Japanese:
- Attendance 4, 105, 108, 114
- Population 26, 29, 30

Jedi Knights, population 36
Jeruma-Grinberga, Rt Revd Jana Jeruma 14
Jesuits 136
Jesus House for all Nations 75, 145
Jewish population 21, 36.37, 41, 42, 43
Jewish synagogues 46
JIM campaign 134
Jinadu, Rev Dr P 137
Joining the church 38
Jordan, Revd Stuart 14

Keller, Dr Tim 14
Kensington & Chelsea 21, 42, 43, 66, 76, 91, 92
Kensington Temple 75, 137
Kings Cross 31
Kingston upon Thames 67, 70, 72, 92
Kingsway International Christian Centre 69, 75
Korean:
- Attendance 4, 105, 108, 114
- Population 26, 29, 30, 31

Lady of Huntingdon's Connexion 46
Lambeth 21, 25, 33, 43, 47, 66, 68, 69, 72, 76, 132
Langham Partnership 133, 141
Langley Chapel 137
Languages spoken 28
Larger churches 3, 4, 55, 62, 69, 73, 75, 111, 146, 147
Latin 30
Latvian 29
Lay-led leadership 138
Leadership 97, 137, 148
Legion of Mary 136

Length of attendance 109, 155
Length of service 101
Lewisham 21, 25, 66, 69, 76
Lewisham High Street 19
Liberal:
Age of churchgoers 89, 90
Age of ministers 153
Attendance 64, 65, 76
Churches 32
Community activity 126
Distance from church 111
Ethnicity 108
Length of attendance 109, 110, 155
Worshippers 5
Lincoln's Inn 11
Lingala (Congo) 30
Lithuanian 29, 30
Living Waters Foursquare Church 137
Local Ecumenical Partnerships 17, 60, 135
London City Mission 1,3, 46, 145
London Diocese – *see* Diocese of London
Losses in numbers 83, 84
Low Church:
Age of churchgoers 89, 90
Age of ministers 153
Attendance 64, 65
Churches 32, 58
Community activity 126
Distance from church 111
Ethnicity 108
Length of attendance 109,155
Lunch Clubs 122
Lutheran Churches 17, 60

Mainstream Evangelical:
Age of churchgoers 89, 90
Age of ministers 153
Attendance 64, 65
Churches 32
Community activity 126
Distance from church 111
Ethnicity 108
Growth 65
Length of attendance 109, 155
Targetting membership 139
Malayalam 30, 31
Male attendance 49, 80, 81, 117, 151, 152
Maltese 29
Mandarin (Chinese) 30
MARC Europe 163
Marginalised people 140
Marylebone 47
Mass midweek 115
Masters, Dr Peter 58
Media action 126, 156
Men under 20 5
Merton 21, 25, 33, 67, 70, 72
Message of the Hour 136
Messy Church 146
Methodist Church:
Age of attenders 95, 152
Age of ministers 153
Attendance 49, 57
Church of Great Britain 16, 59
Churches 23, 47, 88, 89, 124
Closures 58
Community activity 127, 128
Deaths 38
Distance from church 111
Ethnicity 106, 107, 154
Leadership 99, 102, 138
Length of attendance 109, 114, 155
Mid-week 115,118
Planting 24, 140
Translated services 30
Youth activities 120, 121
Metropolitan Tabernacle 58
Mid-week activities 6, 115, 148
Military chapels 16
Missionary-led 138
Mixed ethnicity 25, 105, 106, 154, 155
Monthly attendance 103
Moorgate workers 140
Moral Christians 39
Mormon churches 46
Mosque, large 70
Mother congregation offshoot 135
Motorcyclists 44
Mountain Fire Churches 17
MSC (France) 136
Muddie-Smith, Richard 48
Multiple responsibility 99, 103, 113, 125
Museums 4, 10, 35, 36, 37, 41, 42, 44,

50, 51, 76, 147
Mustard-Seed Foundation Home Mission 136
Muswell Hill 31

Neighbourhood visitation 126, 156
New Churches:
Age of attenders 95, 102, 152
Age of ministers 153
Attendance 49, 57
Churches 23, 47, 88, 89, 124
Community activity 127, 128
Distance from church 111
Ethnicity 106, 107, 154
Groups 16, 59
Large churches 63
Length of attendance 109, 155
Mid-week 115,118
Planting 24, 137, 139, 140
Renting 6
Started 21
Translated services 30
Youth activities 120, 121
Youth worker 100
New Covenant Church, Brixton 137
New Jerusalem churches 50
New Testament church of God 17, 60
Newfrontiers 16, 137
Newham 21, 25, 27, 33, 42, 43, 51, 66, 68, 69, 70, 130, 132
Nicene Creed 65
Nicholls, Dr John 1
Nichols, The Most Revd Vincent 14
Nicoll, Dr Robertson 47
Nigerian 29, 30, 70, 75
No children in church 86
No religion population 36, 37, 40, 41, 42
No teenagers in church 86
Non-attenders 40
Non-religious 40
Non-worship activities 122
Northolt 31
Norwegian 29
Not stated population 36, 37, 41, 42
Number at start 137

O2 Arena 10
Old Roman Catholic Church 16
Older people 82
Olympic Games 9, 13, 69
Ong, Revd Siew Huat 14
Orchestras 10
Ordained leaders 6, 100, 113
Orthodox:
Age of attenders 95, 102, 152
Age of ministers 153
Attendance 49, 57, 129
Churches 23, 47, 88, 89, 124
Community activity 127, 128
Distance from church 111
Ethnicity 106, 154
Groups 16, 31, 59
Large churches 63
Length of attendance 109, 155
Mid-week 115,118
Planting 24, 138
Translated services 30
Youth activities 120
Youth worker 100
Other churchmanships 32, 64, 89, 90, 108, 109, 111, 126, 153, 155
Other religions population 36, 37, 41, 42, 43
Outer London 3, 19, 49, 67, 68, 70, 72, 79, 81, 94, 108, 114, 115, 120, 131, 139, 140, 148
Ownership of churches 124

Pagan population 36
Paid leadership 100
Pakistani population 25
Paralympics 13
Part-time leadership 100, 113, 138
Pentecostal:
Age of attenders 95, 152
Age of ministers 153
Attendance 49, 57
Churches 23, 47, 62, 88, 89, 124
Community activity 127, 128
Distance from church 111
Ethnicity 106, 107, 154
Groups 17, 60
Growth 21, 75
Leadership 148
Length of attendance 109, 155
Mid-week 6, 115,118
Multiple leadership 99

Pentecostal (contd):
Numerous 33
Other religion 130
Planting 7, 24, 99, 134, 137, 138, 140
Renting 6
Translated services 30
Youth activities 5, 120, 121
Youth worker 100
Persian 30
Phelps, Martin 137
Plumstead 1, 58, 98
Polish 28, 29, 57
Political action 126, 156
Population of London 9, 79
Portuguese 29, 30, 139
Powell, Bishop Wilton R 15
Praise Chapel International 137
Public transport 51
Punjabi 30

Quakers – *see* Religious Society of Friends
Quarterly attendance 104

Rail passengers 44
Rastafarian population 36
Ravidassian population 36
Realist population 37
Redbridge 42, 43, 51, 67, 70, 91, 92
Redeemed Christian Church of God 17, 21, 60, 145
Reformation, the 11
Regular attenders 104
Religion, another 130
Religious Society of Friends 17, 46, 60, 140
Rental length 125
Rhea 29
Rhema Bible Training Centre 136
Richmond upon Thames 43, 51, 67, 129
Risk-takers 83
Roehampton University 22
Roman Catholics:
Age of attenders 95, 152
Age of ministers 153
Attendance 49, 57
Churches 23, 47, 62, 88, 89, 124
Community activity 127, 128
Deaths 38
Distance from church 111
Ethnicity 106, 107, 154
Indian attendance 121
Leadership 99, 102
Length of attendance 48, 109, 155
Mid-week 6, 115,118
Multiple services 103
Numerous 16, 75
Planting 99, 140
Specialist churches 146
Translated services 30
Youth activities 121
– *see also* Catholic
Roman invasion 10
Romanian 29, 30, 139
Romford Evangelical 58
Rominger, Revd Roberta 15
Roxeth 31
Ruach Ministries 75, 145
Russian 29, 30, 31
Rwandan 30

Salem Church 137
Salvation Army 17, 50, 60
School attendance 17, 91
School, Harrow 70
Self-supporting churches 7, 142
Senior citizens 140
Serbian 30
Serbo-Croatian 30
Services, number of 6
Seventh-Day Adventists 17, 60
Sexual activity 80
Shadwell 31
Shard, The 11
Shepherd's Bush 31
Shona (Zimbabwe) 30
Sierra Leone 136
Sign language (for the deaf) 30
Sikh population 36, 37, 41, 42, 43
Single parent families 83
Sinhalese (Sri Lanka) 30
Sinnaovrai, Jenny 137
Size of church 55, 61, 72, 86, 87, 107, 118, 128, 154, 156
Slade, The, 58
Slovak 29, 30

Smaller churches 73, 75
Smaller Denominations:
Age of attenders 152
Age of ministers 153
Attendance 49, 57, 129
Churches 23, 47, 62, 88, 89, 124
Community activity 127, 128
Distance from church 111
Ethnicity 106, 107, 154
Groups 17, 60
Leadership 102
Length of attendance 109, 155
Mid-week 115,118
Other religion 130
Planting 7, 99, 134, 137
Translated services 30
Youth activities 121
Smoking by young people 80
Social needs 126, 156
Sookhdeo, Patrick 36
Soul, belief in 40
South Africa 28, 30, 136
Southall 31
Southall Praise 63
Southwark 10, 21, 25, 33, 47, 66, 68, 69, 72, 76, 132
Southwark for Jesus 22
Spanish 28, 29, 30, 31, 139
Specialist churches 111, 146
Spiritual, people who are 40
Spiritualists population 36
Sri Lanka 30
St Anne's, Limehouse 137
St Botolph's, Aldersgate 137
St Helen's, Bishopsgate 75, 92, 135, 137, 146
St Paul's Cathedral 10
St Paul's, Shadwell 137
St Stephen's, Twickenham 137
Stratford 70
Street evangelism 126, 156
Students 10, 140
Summerton, Dr Neil 15
Sunday and mid-week attendance 122
Sunday School attendance 86
Sunday services 102
Sutton 67
Swahili 29
Swedenborgian New Churches 46
Swedish 29
Swiss 29
Syrian 29

Taiwanese 30
Tamil 29, 30, 31, 139
Taoist population 36
Target membership 139
Tate Modern 10
Taxi passengers 44
Teaching courses 156
Teaching crucial 146
Teenage attendance 87
Terrorist attacks 11
Thai 29
Theocharous, The Most Revd Gregorios 15
Theology of planting 143
Third Age 79
Tower Bridge 11, 13
Tower Hamlets 5, 21, 42, 43, 47, 51, 66, 72, 91, 92
Trafalgar Square 11, 31
Trans-Atlantic Alliance of Churches 136
Transient workers in Clapham 139
Translation of services 30
Transport problems 12
Transsexuals 77
Travel in London 5, 33, 44, 111, 112, 146
Travers, Tony 117
Tridentine Institute church 16
Twenties churchgoers 82, 94
Twicers 48

Uganda 30
Ukrainian 29
Unchurched 140
Under 20s in church 85
Underground passengers 44
Unique features 147
Unitarian churches 46, 50
United Pentecostal Church of GB 17
United Reformed Church:
Age of attenders 95, 152
Age of ministers 138, 153
Attendance 49, 57, 102
Churches 23, 47, 88, 89, 124
Closures 24

United Reformed Church (contd):
Community activity 127, 128
Distance from church 111
Ethnicity 106, 154
Groups 17, 60
Leadership 99
Length of attendance 109, 114, 155
Mid-week 115,118
Planting 136
Translated services 30
Youth activities 120, 121
Youth worker 100
– *see also* URC in the text
Universities, number 10
Urban Expression 136
Urdu 28, 29, 31, 139

Vietnamese 29
Viking attacks 10, 97
Vineyard churchesc136
Virginity 80
Visitors 9, 103

Wales, numbers in 36, 37
Walkers 44
Waltham Forest 25, 42, 51, 67, 91, 92, 95, 129
Wandsworth 21, 25, 66, 69
Wanstead inhabitants 139
Warren, Rick 137
Weekly attendance 103, 113
Wembley 31
Westminister, City of 5, 11, 47, 51, 66, 69, 76, 91, 92, 119, 129, 130, 132
Westminster Chapel 58
White:
Churchgoers 4, 105, 106, 114, 154, 155
Population 25
Wicca population 36
William the Conqueror 97
William, King 11
Wimbledon 12
Women attenders 5
Woodhead, Prof Linda 39, 40
Woolwich 75
World War bombing 97
Wren, Sir Christopher 11

Xhosa (South Africa) 30

Year appointed as leader 101, 113
Year church started 97
Yoruba (Nigerian) 30
Young people's activities 120
Youth club 120
Youth in church 85
Youth ministry 7
Youth workers 6, 100, 113

Zambian 29
Zimbabwe 29, 30
Zoroastrian population 36

For contact details please see previous page

UK Church Statistics
Number 2 2010 -2020

This volume is a fresh updated compilation of the number of members, churches and ministers in the many denominations in the UK, with summary tables, explanatory articles and other data. It gives a detailed denomination by denomination overview of church membership, churches and congregations and the number of ministers (including gender).

It covers each year from 2010 to 2020 with a forecast, often provided by the individual denomination itself, of numbers in 2020. The Introduction draws out the major trends and items of importance from this mass of data.

There are an estimated 340 different denominations in the UK, by far the largest proportion being those which are Pentecostal, particularly black groups. These denominations are grouped together in 10 broad categories – Anglican, Baptist, Roman Catholic, Independent, Methodist, New Churches, Orthodox, Pentecostal, Presbyterian and Smaller Denominations.

In addition there is a section giving detailed information on the London Church Census, giving details of numbers of churches by denomination, religion, size of congregation, trends in numbers attending, age of churchgoers, and so on, with maps for each Borough in Greater London.

There are also sections giving the numbers of churches by denomination and English county, and church attendance from 1989 through to 2012 by Local or Unitary Authority, ethnic group by religion, different countries across the world as well as world totals, and various essays on key topics. There is also a comprehensive 1,000-entry index.

The value of the volume is that it gives you the latest data at your finger-tips in an easily accessible and readable mode. Graphs and charts illuminate the figures throughout, and the forward-looking estimates give valuable indications of likely trends (both positive and negative). Every known accessible denomination was contacted.